E-10

FIGHTER WRITER

FIGHTER WRITER

The eventful life of Sergeant Joe Lee,
Scotland's forgotten war poet

BOB BURROWS

breedon **books**
PUBLISHING

Dedication

Dedicated to the memory of my late mother, Emily Maria Burrows, and to my first grandchild, Emily Grace Burrows, born April 2004.

First published in Great Britain in 2004 by
The Breedon Books Publishing Company Limited
Breedon House, 3 The Parker Centre,
Derby, DE21 4SZ.

ISBN 1 85983 399 5

Printed and bound by Butler & Tanner,
Frome, Somerset, England.

Cover printing by Lawrence-Allen Colour Printers,
Weston-super-Mare, Somerset, England.

Contents

List of poems

This list only includes those poems that are quoted in full within the text. Many others are quoted in part.

Acknowledgements and Sources

In telling the life story of Joe Lee I am indebted to the people at the University of Dundee, the staff at D.C. Thomson, particularly David Torrie and Tom Stewart, the staff at the *Dundee Advertiser* and Thomas B. Smyth, archivist at The Black Watch Museum in Perth. Peter Bates at J. & J. Tod in Peover provided some of the First World War photographs. Thanks are also due to John and Nancy Hughes for their unflagging support, and, most of all, to Joe's niece Kathleen Blackwood, for her enthusiasm and incredible memory.

Among the many works I consulted during the writing of this book, the following were particularly helpful:

Goodbye to All That, Robert Graves
The Poet of Dundee, R.J.B. Sellar
The Scottish Regiments, Patrick Mileham
A History of the Black Watch, A.G. Wauchope
The Autobiography of a Journalist and *The Haunting Years*, Sir Linton Andrews
Memoirs of an Infantry Officer, Siegfried Sassoon

Joe Lee's published works, *Ballads of Battle* and *Work-a-day Warriors*, published by John Murray, *A Captive at Carlsruhe*, published by John Lane, The Bodley Head, and *Tales O' Our Town*, published by George Montgomery, are referred to extensively and extracts are reproduced by permission of the copyright holder.

Introduction

IT WAS early October 1998 when I came across a small, brown book. Little did I realise, as I picked it up, that it would launch me on a three-year quest. My mother had died and it had fallen to me as the eldest son to act as executor and to sort out her financial and personal effects in keeping with her last wishes. As anyone who has performed this task will know, it is an emotional process sifting through and throwing away items which have meant so much to the family.

There were no riches to speak of among my mother's things, just a wealth of memories. It was while throwing away old magazines and allocating books to be delivered to local charities that the small brown book, *Ballads of Battle* by Sergeant Joe Lee of the Black Watch, caught my eye.

Flicking casually through the pages, I was at first struck by the beautiful sketches that illustrated the Scottish poems. Perhaps I was feeling vulnerable, having lost my much-loved mother, but I paused at a poem entitled 'The Mother'.

THE MOTHER
'Mother o' mine; O Mother o' mine.'

My mother rose from her grave last night,
    And bent above my bed,
And laid a warm kiss on my lips,
    A cool hand on my head;
And, 'Come to me, and come to me,
    My bonnie boy,' she said.

* * * * *

And when they found him at the dawn,
    His brow with blood defiled,
And gently laid him in the earth
    They wondered that he smiled.

Emotional, I squatted on the floor and started to read the other poems of life in the trenches during the First World War: of leave and the longing for home, of the characters, artefacts and gore. Eventually, as I turned the last page, moved to silence, I realised that I hadn't even noticed the encroaching darkness – I was lost in Joseph Lee's world.

It was probably a year later that I returned to the little book, which I had placed in my own collection, determined to find out more about the writer. I had at first thought that it would be a relatively easy task to ascertain who he was and whether he had written and illustrated other books. Yet trawling through the reference sections of various libraries, and scanning the Internet, drew a virtual blank. In only one single reference book I discovered a tantalising reference to Joseph Lee, which turned out later to have both his date of birth and date of death wrong, and which quoted only one of his many poems.

The breakthrough came when I contacted the Black Watch archivist, Thomas Smyth, in Perth. He knew of Lee as 'the Black Watch poet' and pointed me in the direction of Dundee University, where I discovered a treasure trove of Lee's other publications, letters, journals and photographs. Further detective work led me to two living relatives of Joe Lee: Miss Kathleen Blackwood, a niece, and Mrs Nancy Hughes, a great

John and Nancy Hughes and Kathleen Blackwood, surviving relatives of Joe Lee.

niece. Together with Nancy's husband John they were very supportive and helpful, both on my visits to Dundee and in response to questions raised by my research.

As my work continued, I discovered that Lee was a man of integrity and honesty whose talents were bountiful. Artist, poet, journalist, traveller, soldier and prisoner of war, his life was full and also encompassed a great love for his home town, Dundee, and a great love for a woman, Dorothy Barrie. I uncovered intriguing reasons, which will be explained at length, why his fame has not endured and why his talents have long gone unrecognised.

My association with Joe Lee began with a personal tragedy, the death of my mother, and the three years I have spent uncovering his story have been cathartic – it has felt as if I were meant to tell his tale to a new generation of readers who will not have come across him in their studies of the poets of the First World War. I hope to be able to communicate my enthusiasm for his work, and to convince my readers that it is high time that Lee was looked at in his proper context and his talent recognised in the way it so richly deserves.

Bob Burrows
May 2004

Prologue

JUNE 1815, Hougoumont, Waterloo:

Sergeant David Lee's gaze swept the battlefield as he waited anxiously for the next French cavalry charge to overwhelm the British artillery.

Positioned on Wellington's right, the British forces, which included Lee's Royal Horse Artillery, had since 11.30am faced a major assault by Napoleon's troops. Several times the French lancers had swept over the British positions but had failed to spike their guns, an omission which was to prove costly. As each charge breached their position the gunners retreated behind the British infantry squares, only to re-emerge to recharge their guns for another salvo as the attack subsided. Despite heavy losses Gunner Lee's Royal Horse Artillery managed to keep up a steady bombardment, which eventually helped to break the French. The failure of the French to spike the British guns perhaps cost them the victory at Waterloo. Sergeant Lee saw the massed ranks of French infantry, resplendent in their blue tunics, white trousers and distinctive white criss-cross bandoliers, marching to the insistent, rhythmic beat of dozens of drums and to their certain deaths as the British and their allies poured musket and artillery fire into their ranks. When the huge, dense clouds of smoke which covered and drifted over the conflict after every massive salvo eventually cleared, he could see the huge gaps that had been scythed through the seething, squirming mass of humanity.

Despite acts of chivalry fighting was vicious, savage and at times hand-to-hand, with bayonets and swords. Casualties on both sides were estimated at 60,000. The battlefield was a massive junkyard of broken bodies; wounded men crying out for assistance; dead and dying horses; carnage and gore.

* * * * *

September 1915, the Western Front:

Sergeant Joseph Lee of the 4th Battalion, The Black Watch had just completed seven months in France and his battalion had experienced action at Festubert, Neuve Chapelle, Aubers Ridge and the Battle of Loos, where they had suffered horrendous losses. He had watched and fought as the Germans advanced over open ground in the face of devastating fire from machine guns and artillery, which cut them down in their thousands. The British and their French allies had also been ravaged as they in turn advanced on German positions. Fighting had been fierce and brutal, and there had been hand-to-hand encounters with bayonets, knives and swords.

The battlefields were strewn with corpses, the broken bodies of the wounded and dying, bloated horse carcasses and shattered machinery. Smoke from the guns blinded the eyes, while the smell of cordite stung nostrils and clouds of mustard gas destroyed lungs, drifting over and enveloping the awful scenes.

* * * * *

The hundred years between the two conflicts had seen little change apart from the fact that the protagonists had changed sides. At Waterloo the Germans fought with the British against the French and in the First World War the British and French fought the Germans.

However, for the Lee family it was a question of history repeating itself. Gunner Sergeant David Lee was the grandfather of Sergeant, later Lieutenant, Joseph Lee of Dundee, famed as 'the Black Watch poet'. Joe Lee wrote a poem on the front line in Flanders in 1915, which he called '1815–1915: One Hundred Years Ago To-day' and he dedicated it to his grandfather and his four paternal aunts. It was later featured in his published book *Ballads of Battle.*

1815–1915
ONE HUNDRED YEARS AGO TO-DAY

TO MY GRANDFATHER
WHO FOUGHT AT WATERLOO

Affectionately Dedicated to
my Four Paternal Aunts

Once more the unsheathed sword, once more the speeding
    shell;
Once more unleashing of the Hounds of Hell;
The Nations rage together, and again
The Kings are joined for battle on the plain;
Old Europe armed goes forth to smite and slay,
Just as a Hundred Years to-day!

Grandsire, whom I have never seen nor held whose hand,
Nor heard whose voice – stentorian in command –
From some Valhalla of the British dead
Perchance thou watchest where our lines are spread:
Strengthen my hand; thy kinsman's heart inspire
With some spark of thy ancient martial fire –
May my steel be as keen, I pray,
As yours, a Hundred Years to-day!

Oft as a boy I strove to swing thy blade
From out the scabbard where it long had laid,
And fearful felt the edge – the notch, 'twas said,
Was compliment from a dead Chasseur's head –
And all day waged the mimic fight,
Waiting for Blucher – and nurse! – and night:
Thank God! I see the children play
As I did – was it Yesterday?

I hear your guns growl on through Spain,
And then I hear them once again
Take up the old terrific tune
Upon that far-off Eighteenth June
Mine ears have learned the measure well
At Festubert and Neuve Chapelle –
Our friends, forth with us in this fray,
Were foes a Hundred Years to-day!

When you rode through this war-racked land
Didst ever, prithee, kiss a hand
To Jeanne, Yvonne, Marcelle, Marie –
Grand-dames of those wave hands to me?
Were girls as sportive and as gay? –
Didst have the heart to say them Nay? –
Was't easy parting with thy pay
A Hundred Years Ago to-day?

* * * * *

Grandsire, whose good right hand is long since dust,
I hold the same true steel in sacred trust;
From some Valhalla of the British dead
Perchance thou watchest where our lines are spread
Thou knewest whence should come the power
When dark the battle-clouds did lower –
May thy God be my shield and stay
As thine a Hundred Years to-day!

FLANDERS, 18th June, 1915.

The poem recounts the similarities between the conflicts taking place a century apart, but Joe Lee does note the historic irony of the fact that although the combatants are the same, they have changed sides: 'Our friends forth with us in this fray,/Were foes a Hundred Years to-day!'.

Although Joseph Lee never knew his grandfather he clearly had respect for him, and in his imagination he forged a bond with him, which bridged the years. Crouched in a trench in Flanders in 1915, vulnerable and apprehensive, Lee reached back through the years for strength and support from his ancestor.

At one point in Joseph Lee's life, in 1904, depressed, out of work and penniless, he was moved to enlist in the army and recalled that it was 100 years ago to the month since his grandfather also enlisted. He remembered examining David Lee's Waterloo and Peninsular campaign medals, holding his sword and his flint and steel holster pistol and envying his experiences. This childhood fantasy is also remembered in the poem. However, in the event Lee's own enlistment in the army would be deferred for another 10 years.

CHAPTER ONE

The Lee Family

DAVID Lee, Joseph Lee's grandfather, must have been a remarkable
man. His father had been a soldier in the Royal Dragoons and David
Lee enlisted in the Royal Horse Artillery at the age of 16 and survived 19
engagements in the Peninsular War, retiring with the rank of sergeant at
the age of 35. He had the rare distinction of earning the General Service
Medal and 10 bars. The medals are on display in Dundee Museum, and
his Waterloo sword is at Broughty Ferry Castle. Some of his characteristics
seem to have been inherited by his grandson, and an incident in his life
illustrates something of the character that manifested itself in Joe Lee in
later years.

David Lee, having fought at Waterloo, also fought in one of the
bloodiest encounters in British military history. During the Peninsular
War the British, under Wellington, supported by Portuguese troops,
besieged the Spanish fortress town of Badajoz on 6 April 1812. The
fighting was ferocious and eventually the 'impregnable' fortress fell to the
British, but at great cost of life. Anglo-Portuguese casualties were over
5,000 and the French defenders lost 1,500. The British forces, in a betrayal
of the renowned British discipline, fuelled by alcohol and sickened by the
loss of so many friends, ransacked the city in a frenzy of rape, looting,
murder and fire. Any sign of resistance from the local populace was settled
by bayonet or bullet. Events escalated out of control and when British
officers were subjected to assaults from their own troops, Wellington
ordered that gallows be erected and threatened that further indiscipline
would be punished with executions.

During this unrest Sergeant David Lee showed great courage and commendable spirit when he saved a young Spanish girl from his drunken colleagues. Hearing a woman's screams coming from a burning building, Lee, sword in hand, raced into the flickering flames. Drunken British soldiers had cornered a young woman. Lee warned that he would kill the first man to touch her and, despite their threats to kill him, he restored order and got her to safety. Later on in the Peninsular campaign he married her. It was this same spirit of justice, determination and high principles that so characterised Joe Lee's life.

However, the Spanish girl was not to be Joe Lee's grandmother. Sadly she fell ill and died, and when David Lee eventually returned to Dundee he married Hermonina, a sister of Joseph Johnston, founder of the well-known Dundee fishing business, and she was Joe Lee's grandmother. Her family name, Johnston, became Joseph Lee's middle name. It was the custom in her family to name female children after male relatives, leading to such names as Williamina, Johnina, Georgina and of course the tongue-twister Hermonina. The family eventually tired of grappling with these formalities and changed the tradition so that later female descendants were known as Ina, Nina, Ena, and Nena, which were easier to pronounce but just as confusing.

Official records show that David and Hermonina had four children: David Alexander Lee, born 11 August 1843; Hermonina Margaret Johnston Lee, born 10 January 1846; George-Ann Jemima Lee, born 15 June 1847; and Harriet Elliot Lee, born 16 February 1851, all born in Montrose. However, in 1915 Joe Lee specifically dedicated his poem '1815–1915: One Hundred Years Ago To-day' to his grandfather and his four paternal aunts! Despite exhaustive research the elusive fourth paternal aunt remains a mystery. Hermonina Margaret Johnston and her sister George-Ann had a joint wedding in July 1870 and Harriet married in 1875.

David Alexander Lee, a draper's assistant, married a pregnant Christina Easson Blair in Perth on 6 February 1866. Their first-born David, imaginatively named in the family tradition, arrived on 17 May 1866 and thereafter a child was born every two years. Nelly was born in 1868, Andrew Blair in 1870, Herman Johnston in 1872, Minnie in 1874, Joseph

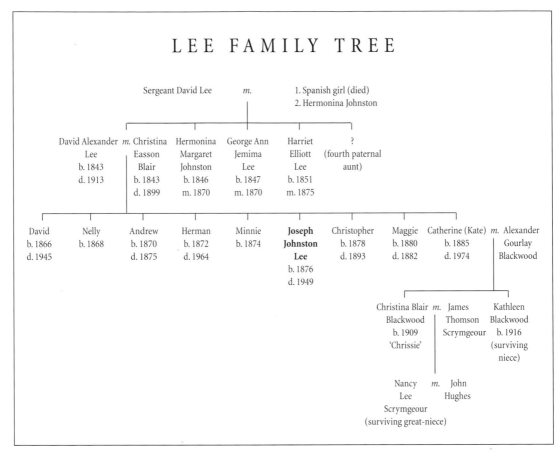

LEE FAMILY TREE

The Lee family tree.

(Joe) Johnston in 1876, Christopher in 1878 and Maggie in 1880. Catherine Blair (Kate) broke the sequence when she arrived in 1885. All the children were born in Dundee and for a time the family lived in Hedge Road before moving into tenements in the Wellgate area.

Of David and Christina's nine children, six survived, while typically for the period three children died young. Andrew Blair Lee was the first of the children to die in 1875. An apparently bright, healthy toddler, it is believed that he succumbed to whooping cough at the age of five. This tragic loss was slightly compensated for by the birth of Joseph Johnston Lee, who was born in Dundee on 6 December 1876. Sadly, as was the case with many British Victorian families, disease and death were never far away. Joe Lee was only six years old when his sister Maggie died aged two in 1882. The Howff burial ground in the centre of Dundee bears ample testimony to the mortality rate of children under the age of 10 in those days. In some instances families lost two, three, or four children, and in one tragic family there are seven recorded deaths of infants.

In terms of world history 1876 was interesting, if relatively uneventful. George Custer, soldier, departed this life at the Little Big Horn, Wild Bill Hickock, cowboy, was shot dead in Deadwood, and the restless free spirit Geronimo was roaming around and terrorising Mexico. Mark Twain wrote *The Adventures of Tom Sawyer* and Renoir painted *Au Moulin de la Galette*. Joe Lee, later soldier, cowboy, restless free spirit, writer and artist, might have thought these events coincidental but somehow fitting. In his home town, Dundee, the Tay rail bridge, which Lee would come to know well, was half constructed at the time of his birth in 1876. It was completed in 1878 but then in 1879, on a cold winter's night, 90 people died when the bridge collapsed as a train was crossing.

Joe Lee's father, David Lee, worked in Spence's high-class draper's shop, which is believed to have been on the site of Boots the chemist today. He was in charge of the button department, which meant that he was responsible for the stocking and ordering of all the various types, designs, colours and quantities. Buttons at that time were highly fashionable items, not merely functional but also decorative. Nevertheless, the boring and repetitive nature of the daily routine offered little in the way of challenge or satisfaction for David. As the years went by he became frustrated and dissatisfied with his lot. Inevitably he vented his frustration at home, turning to drink and embarking on an inevitable downward spiral into argument, abuse and confrontation.

He may have believed that he was a disappointment to his wife Christina and that he had somehow failed her. Her family, the Blairs, were comparatively well off. Half the family were doctors, while the women of the family married doctors, and another relative owned a chemist's shop. Christina herself was sensitive, hard working and conscientious. Before her marriage she had been a seamstress, spending long days at a sewing machine braiding jackets, waistcoats and coats. Her skills stood her in good stead as their family increased and she was constantly called upon to repair or make garments out of remnants and scraps of material. She found the work therapeutic and was able to forget her worries as she struggled to satisfy her family's needs. She was a good wife and mother and undeserving of the hardships that were inevitable in an overcrowded tenement dwelling in Wellgate, a run-down, sordid part of the town, with a husband who was disenchanted with his life, drinking and arguing with his two older sons.

David, or Dave as he was known, born in 1865, was a restless, strong-willed and determined character. No doubt provoked by the atmosphere at home, he engaged in drunken arguments with his father and brother Herman. Moody and aggressive after a few drinks, Dave had difficulty holding down a job, although he was a talented man. He had spells as a chemist in Dundee, became a dentist and for a year travelled as a ship's doctor on a whaling ship. Most of the medical treatment on board was routine, but when whaling operations were in full swing more serious cases had to be faced. Severe lacerations and broken limbs tested his talents and he lived up to expectations. Indeed, on one whaling trip they landed on a tiny island where scurvy was rife among the natives. With his medical knowledge and pharmaceutical skills, Dave managed to cure them, and in gratitude they presented him with a carved walking stick. He eventually emigrated to Canada, where he lived until his death in 1945.

Like his elder brother, Herman, the second son, took a dim view of life and felt that he too had been dealt a dud hand. He had good reason, for he was regarded as a clever lad, maybe even university material. However, like Dave before him and Joe after him, there was no money available for education and the boys were expected to go to work. Herman did buckle down for a while, joining a large wholesale firm in Dundee and eventually working his way up to chief cashier. However, it was not long before he became frustrated and turned to the bottle. Yet despite his drink habit, which bordered on alcoholism, and frequent warnings about a shortened life expectancy, Herman died in 1964 at the grand old age of 92.

The atmosphere in the cramped tenement dwelling, with three male adults, all strong-willed characters, who were at times drunk and argumentative, was terrifying for the younger members of the family. There is no evidence to suggest that Christina was ever physically abused, but she was constantly protective of her younger children and tried to calm the warring factions. She did have a strong ally, a real bundle of energy, in her oldest daughter, Nelly. Nelly was a tough character who kept the younger siblings in order, sometimes with just a piercing look. Her niece, Kathleen Blackwood, remembers her telling her that whenever she went out to play she always had to take the younger members of the family with her. She would be turning one end of a skipping rope with one arm while carrying a baby or toddler in the other. She remembered that Joe Lee was the heaviest as he was such a chubby boy.

Nelly did not have much of a childhood and was soon sent out to work. Her first job was as an apprentice to a shroud-maker. Crouching over a busy sewing machine, with yards of billowing white material around her, she would hoist it over her left shoulder as she moved on to the hemming. She later spent time working with a milliner stitching braid round straw hats, and then she went on to dress-making. Her apprenticeship often involved boring jobs, such as unpicking the seams of garments to enable them to be 'turned', a process by which the worn and faded parts of garments were turned to the inside to extend the life of a suit, dress or jacket. Hard times forced such innovation. Nelly's hard-won skills stood her in good stead for the future.

At the age of 18 she commenced employment at a draper's shop which had just opened in Dundee, D.M. Brown's. It was a one-roomed emporium with a cloakroom, which was accessed through a trapdoor set

The site of D.M. Brown's, which later became House of Fraser and then Arnotts. Nelly Lee, Joe's sister, worked there when it was a one-room shop.

in the floor and descending a wooden ladder. Nelly worked very hard helping the company grow and develop and when she retired at the age of 65 she had been the buyer for the children's department for many years. This one-roomed shop eventually became House of Fraser and later Arnotts. Despite her tough upbringing, or maybe because of it, Nelly had a long and active life, dying at the age of 98 having lost none of her faculties.

There is little information about a younger sister, Minnie, whose full name was Williamina Davidson Lee. It is known that at one point she returned to the family home after a failed marriage.

At the age of 43, Christina ended almost 20 years of childbearing when Catherine (Kate) was born in 1885. By then Joe also had a younger brother, Christopher, whom he described as a gentle delicate boy, who had been born with a heart defect, and he doted on both of them.

Kathleen Blackwood, Kate's daughter, remembers that there was a special bond between Christina and two of her younger children, Joe and Kate. These two were both sensitive children, and when they witnessed the drunken arguments between their older brothers and their father they were both terrified and traumatised. Kate was always frightened that her mother would be hurt when intervening to calm them down. There was also the social stigma of going to school and being taunted by neighbours who had heard the previous night's shouting and bawling. In the crowded tenements this was no rare occurrence, but spiteful schoolgirls still took pleasure in chiding the neat, quiet little girl.

Joe, who was afflicted with asthma all of his life, was himself taunted when he began to attend Harris Academy at the age of 11, because he was scholarly and was regarded as a bright lad with a future. When Kate went to the same school some years later, the teachers would say to her 'So you're Joe Lee's sister are you?', the inference being that they wondered how someone as bright as Joe could have a sister like Kate.

Despite his asthma, and despite being a bright intelligent lad who stood out quietly from the crowd, Joe was a normal, mischievous boy. Later, recalling his childhood days in his poetry, he would write of being caned for dodging school, stealing apples, playing football and cricket, being good at draughts and running barefoot round the streets of Dundee with his pals. But sadly Joe suffered the same fate as his older brothers:

although he was considered intelligent and of university standard he was expected to go to work as soon as possible in order to contribute to the family finances. Further education was simply not an option. Times were hard and the family required a contribution from everyone. So Joe left school at the age of 14 and started work in 1890 in the offices of Dundee solicitors D. S. & I. Littlejohn. In the short term he was happy to be working and doing his bit for the family and helping his hard-pressed mother.

Despite the problems there was real love in the family, and they did have good times. Oldest brother Dave went away on his travels, and life for Christina improved as her daughters rallied round her and everyone started to play their part. However, tragedy struck again when Christopher died at the age of 15 in 1893. Although he had been in poor health and his death was not unexpected, it was nevertheless a blow that was felt most keenly. He had always been around while Joe and Kate were growing up and they felt his loss deeply.

Kate started work in 1898 at D.M. Brown's, under the watchful eye of her big sister Nelly. Strictly speaking, as she was only 13 years old, she was illegally employed. Despite her tender years she worked long hours, often returning home to the sometimes dangerous tenements in the dark.

After a reasonably quiet period of steady progress for the family, with most of them working, Dave travelling in Canada and Joe having left Littlejohns to try his luck in London, drawing cartoons for a living and studying art, the family was once again hit hard by a bereavement. Joe's father was taken seriously ill and Joe returned home from London when he found out just how grave the situation was. On 19 January 1899 David Lee passed away in his son Joe's arms. He was only 56. As ever the family rallied round and although Joe continued to travel and work in London, his mother had strong support at home, particularly from Nelly.

Over the next several years the family had a period of relative calm. Joe travelled to several parts of the world, trying his hand at a variety of roles, before returning to take up journalism in his home town. Kate continued to work steadily, and then, on 11 June 1908, she married Alexander Gourlay Blackwood. On 4 April 1909 she gave birth to Christina Blair Blackwood. Christina, or Chrissie as she came to be called, the first grandchild, was named after her grandmother, a gesture which brought great pleasure to Christina Lee. It also turned Joe Lee from a doting older brother to a doting uncle.

There was more pleasure, pride and satisfaction for Christina when Joe Lee dedicated his first book of published poems, *Tales O' Our Town,* to her in 1910. Sadly she did not live to see the birth of her second granddaughter, Kathleen Lee Blackwood (registered as Catherine), who was born to Kate and Alexander on 4 May 1916. Christina died on 30 March 1913 at the age of 70. Although she had had a hard life she had raised a large family in poor circumstances and had the satisfaction of knowing that several of her children had made something of their lives.

When Kate died on 16 December 1974 aged 89 she too was a grandmother. Her daughter Chrissie (Christina) had married James Thomson Scrymgeour, and gave birth on 1 June 1944 to Nancy Lee Scrymgeour, who married John Hughes on 20 July 1990. Kathleen Blackwood is today the sole surviving niece of Joe Lee, while Nancy Hughes is the sole surviving great-niece.

CHAPTER TWO

The Restless Years

JOE Lee did not find the work at Littlejohns either demanding or satisfying. His natural instincts for flair and creativity were being stifled by regime, protocol and formality. Several years as the office junior, performing everyday menial tasks with little opportunity for progress or development, served only to fuel his frustration. Soon his restlessness became wanderlust, a desire to see the world and have new experiences, that was to be a characteristic of his personality for most of his life. The lively, talented teenager whose ambition and talent was being stifled by the daily grind and the struggle to survive, started to look around.

It is believed that on impulse he went to Dundee docks and boarded an old steamer, which was heading for the Bosphorous and thence to the Black Sea. Working his passage as a stoker gave him wonderful opportunities to indulge his natural talent for black and white sketches. He made fine pencilled observations throughout the voyage, of Gibraltar, people, Greek churches, boats on the Bosphorous and life on board ship, which were sketched in a book that has survived unpublished. The sights, sounds and smells of a part of the world with a totally different culture to that of his native Scotland fascinated him. Sailing through the Dardanelles onto Gallipoli and then Constantinople, now Istanbul, gave him the opportunity to briefly explore that historic, exotic city. Passing through the natural waterway of the Bosphorous, linking the Mediterranean with the Black Sea, Lee was able to visit Sebastopol. Situated at the tip of the Crimean peninsular, it brought the opportunity of a visit to the battlefields of the Crimean War. Little did Lee realise, as he surveyed the area in which the Black Watch had fought so gallantly, that he would one day be forever linked with the proud Scottish regiment.

In a just a few short years, however, the serene, beautiful and unique part of the world that Lee voyaged through would be torn apart by human conflict. British and British Empire forces, with French support, would engage Turkish forces in a battle to win the Dardanelles and open a supply route to Russia across the Black Sea. The struggle for Gallipoli, which began in 1915, involved nearly one million men and caused almost half a million casualties. Also in 1915, Lee would be fighting for his own life in a different struggle in northern France.

A voyage to the Baltic Sea yielded exquisite drawings of Russian women washing clothes in streams and of bare-footed Russian lads playing flutes and wearing distinctive tunics and hats. Drawings of a woman carrying milk pails slung from a pole, which was stressed and bending to support the weight, and an old man studiously patching a garment, reveal the artist's gift for detail.

Joe Lee's sketches of another journey, this time along the River Scheldt through Holland, including a trip to Rotterdam, are delightful. Even the obligatory windmills are beautifully drawn in black and white. His observations of landscapes, people, buildings and objects capture moments perfectly. A Dutch boy cycling, wearing sabots and a conical hat; a dog cart; a slouching peasant; a girl carrying a heavy pail with the strain clearly showing; riverside scenes and buildings are captured with all the clarity of a camera. No one, least of all Lee, could know that these peaceful European scenes would be transformed by the ravages of the First World War in the near future. In blissful ignorance of what was to come, the artist plainly enjoyed what he saw. A visit to the zoo in Rotterdam inspired a sketch and a poem on the subject of the polar bear:

A detailed sketch of a windmill and its occupier, drawn by Lee while travelling between Dordrecht and Rotterdam.

> I saw a Bear in Rotterdam
> A-turning in his cage
> He wasn't looking very fierce,
> He wasn't in a rage.
> But still he kept a turning & a turning in his cage
> & a turning & a turning in his cage.

Says Jim

To him – in Rotterdam

Why do you turn around?

Why don't you bathe?

Or sit or stand

Or lie upon the ground.

But always you keep turning &

a turning and a turning

    and

a turning and a turning round.

He never stopped, but

'Jim' he sez, 'I'm turning round about

Just 'cause I am a wearying

and a longing to get out.'

A polar bear in a zoo
in Rotterdam, which
Joe Lee saw on his
travels. The sketch is
accompanied by a
poem, which may be
one of Joe Lee's
earliest works.

After each of his trips, Lee always returned to his beloved Dundee, although Canada threatened to break Dundee's stranglehold on his affections. He simply fell in love with its vastness, its wilderness and its people. A wonderful sketched scene in his notebook suggests that he left for Canada aboard the SS *Yoruba* in July 1902. The drawing shows crew quarters with bunks, one of which is filled by a crewman who appears to have fallen asleep after a few drinks, while another crewman, with his head resting on his hand, is smoking a pipe. The scene is chaotic, with clothes, bottles and detritus everywhere. For Lee, well used to the crowded rooms of the family tenement, such conditions would not be too hard to cope with. Mr

The detailed sketch of life on board the SS *Yoruba*.

Cooper, the second mate on the ship, is depicted playing a banjo in a fine drawing. Judging by the cramped quarters he was guaranteed a captive audience.

The sea voyage safely over, Lee journeyed across Alberta to the small town of Medicine Hat, where he got a job as a cowpuncher on the R.P. Ranch at Stony Creek. He learnt to ride horses, round up cattle, repair fences and earn his keep. In later years he spoke very fondly of this happy period in his life. It was hard work, but the camaraderie, the lifestyle of the great outdoors and the laid-back attitude of his cowboy colleagues had great appeal for him. He has left a self-portrait of himself complete with Stetson and neckerchief. He also left a poem, 'The Sidlaw Hills'. Despite his apparent happiness, Scotland, and in particular Dundee, was always in his heart. The poem was inspired by the view of the Cypress Hills of Alberta, which reminded Lee of his homeland. After almost a year in Canada Lee wrenched himself away and returned home.

THE SIDLAW HILLS

At the sight of the Cypress Range, Alberta

The high hills, the low hills,
    The quiet hills o' hame;
It's O that I were lying there,
Where curlews wild are crying there,
    Far ower the saut sea faem.

The high hills, the low hills,
    Wi' yellow bloom aglow;
It's O, that I were roaming there,
Wi' her, where darkly foaming there,
    The rushing torrents go.

The high hills, the low hills,
    The hills we trod together;
The silver sage-brush groweth here –
But pale to him who knoweth, dear,
    The sight o' purple heather.

O, high hills, O, low hills,
    Ye have my heart in hold;
Where lonely I am dwelling here,
The plains are widely swelling here –
    Give me thy ramparts old.

O, high hills, O, low hills,
    O, fair hills ower the faem;
Where lightly winds are sighing there,
Where high the clouds are flying there,
Where curlews wild are crying there,
It's O, that I were lying there –
    For then were I at hame.

A poignant incident showing the trust and esteem with which Joe Lee was regarded while away on his travels is revealed in a signed letter/note made in his sketchbook. It is written by the Chief Engineer of the steamer SS *Loch Maree*, one of the ships that Lee worked on. Dated 29 June 1903, it states: 'Please give the bearer all letters and telegrams for above named steamer and oblige. Yours truly, Chief Engr. David Gourday.'

A footnote written by Lee says that he was entrusted with this responsibility at Blyth. He adds, 'Poor Gourday was drowned on 31st October 1903.'

* * * * *

During his time spent travelling Lee also managed to spend some time in London. He attended the Slade School of Art in the late 1890s, residing at 2a, Cathcart Studios, South Kensington. It was during this time that he received the news of his father's illness and rushed back to Dundee. His father died in his arms, a daunting and emotional experience for a young man barely 22. He returned to London after his father's death, still seeking an outlet for his talents but not wishing to give up his freedom in exchange for imprisonment in an office or factory. When asked much later in life what his recreational preferences were, despite his many talents, Lee replied, 'going to and fro in the earth and walking up and down doing it.' Wanderlust indeed.

By the age of 28 Lee had not settled down to any permanent occupation. Returning from his last big voyage, he spent some lucrative months in London working as a black and white artist. During this period he was drawing cartoons morning, noon and night for Joe Chamberlain's Tariff Reform League. He was working so hard that the cartoons even began to disturb his dreams.

One night he had a theme vision, which suddenly came into his head. He got up from his bed and completed the drawing. He then set off in the morning and walked all the way to Shaftesbury Avenue from Kensington, to save the bus fare, and collected a cheque for three guineas from the agent.

He remembered that as he waited for the cheque he could hear a barrel organ churning out *Santa Lucia*, and from that moment he always associated that particular piece of music with pleasurable thoughts. He gave the Italian barrel organ owner and his wife a shilling.

Sadly, however, the golden seam of cartoon commissions petered out when the Tariff Reform League ceased to be the provocative issue of the day. Work dried up and Lee found himself in desperate straits. He got out his top hat and morning coat (style indeed!) and toured the city looking for suitable work to help him over his financial problems. He not only drew a blank but he remembers that someone sat on his top hat and damaged it. Desperate and depressed, he headed for St George's Barracks behind the National Gallery, determined to join the army. It was 100 years to the month since his grandfather David Lee had enlisted. When the recruiting sergeant asked Joe which regiment he would like to join, he replied 'Scots Greys'. His time in Canada with horses had given him the confidence to ride with the Greys. Sadly there were no vacancies, but the sergeant offered him a place in his own regiment, the Middlesex Diehards. Just as Lee was about to take the oath, a grey-haired old colonel paused and said, 'You're a Scotsman aren't you? What about a Scottish regiment?' Various regiments were discussed until Joe finally chose the Gordon Highlanders, based in Aberdeen, because it was more remote and further removed from his home town than the Black Watch at Perth.

As Lee waited to be drafted north, a moment of pure Charlie Chaplin humour occurred. Lee recalls that the 'rookies' were assembled for drill and parade, and Lee had to parade wearing his top hat. Mercifully there was no kilt provided. The combination of top hat and kilt would have been ludicrous. However, this inauspicious start to his army career was soon brought to an early end. Fate decreed that it would be a further 10 years before the army could embrace Joe Lee as a volunteer soldier. His family, concerned about his state of mind, despatched his older brother Herman to talk him out of joining the army and offer to buy him out if necessary. An obdurate Lee resisted all such rescue attempts, although he remembers that it grieved him to upset his family.

While these discussions with his family were ongoing, one day, in an uneasy momentary pause, Lee's gaze swept around the tiny studio room where he was living. He spotted what appeared to be a piece of paper caught in the shred of velvet draped over the letter slit in the studio door.

It was a letter, which had been unable to fall through onto the floor and had dangled there undiscovered. Opening the delayed letter was a life-changing moment, for it contained a job offer for a post as a cartoonist and newspaper artist. The letter was from an editor for whom Lee had previously worked. It was to be the start of a career in newspapers, albeit with interruptions, which was to last more than 40 years.

A preliminary interview with the editor gave an accurate foretaste of the chaos, diversity and versatility of the post, something which had not been outlined in the job description. During the interview a reporter broke in to tell the editor that although he had a ticket and a programme for a concert, he had no one available to cover it. The editor turned to Lee. 'Are you interested in music?' he asked. 'Yes' was the reply. 'Then perhaps you would like to cover this for us?' Cartoonist Lee's first career assignment was to report on a performance of *Judas Maccabeus*.

So began a career for which adaptability was essential. Lee's skills with pen and pencil, or sometimes both, were highly prized on a small newspaper with limited staff, and his versatility was worth its weight in gold. He could draw cartoons, produce illustrations for story lines and draw portraits, as well as write reports, features and articles and, in time, sub-edit. His knowledge of art and drama added to his range of critical abilities.

During this period of his life he particularly enjoyed being called upon to act as drama critic, and he had the ability and the range to cover reviews from Shakespeare to Shaw. As any report writer knows, having written the article you are at the mercy of the printer. In 1906 Lee was delighted to travel to Rotterdam to report on the week-long celebrations for Rembrandt's tercentenary. Opening the newspaper in Amsterdam, anxious to see his article in print, he read that it was headed 'From our Special Correspondent in Antwerp' while Rembrandt's painting, 'The Syndice of the Cloth Hall', was referred to as 'The Syndicate'. Lee was livid at the misrepresentation. Nevertheless, his wide range of duties prepared him for greater challenges in the future. He spent more than a year in the fiction department, where he said that the fiction was stranger than truth, and he interspersed that with long spells at the sub-editor's desk, where the truth was stranger than fiction.

Despite the variety and the success of his work in London, Lee found that he missed his home town, and in late 1906 he returned to Dundee, but this time with a career to pursue. He started to produce, edit and write several local magazines: the *City Echo*, *The Tocsin* and the *Piper O' Dundee*. The *City Echo* in particular was a great success. Lee produced this monthly magazine virtually single-handedly for five years, from 1907 to 1912. Typically it would feature poetry, theatre reviews, adverts, local news, pen portraits, book reviews, obituaries, commentary on a variety of local and national issues, cartoons and illustrated jokes. Lee wrote most of the pieces himself and indeed supplied most of the pen and pencil sketches. To achieve the standard he did for five years was a prodigious feat that demonstrated once again his all-round ability. The Dundee University archives have a complete set of the *City Echo*, which is well worth studying. His talents soon came to the attention of John Leng & Company, an important Dundee publishing house, and in 1909 he joined their staff. At this time Lee was also writing poetry, mainly about his home town Dundee, which was regularly published in *The People's Journal*. At Leng's his many talents were again put to good use and he assumed the role of music and art critic.

Criticism is of course subjective, although critics must do their best to be impartial and honest, but this is not always appreciated by the writer or producer who has been on the receiving end of a bad review. On one occasion Joe Lee was made very aware of the danger he courted when ruffling feathers. After being particularly scathing about one production he was warned that the producer was looking for him, armed with a loaded revolver. The following night the offended producer denounced Lee from the stage, arguing that Lee had spent most of the night drinking in the bar, and could not possibly have had a fair view of the play. Lee retorted indignantly that he had viewed the play with his sister, who was teetotal. Reviewing another production, *Hush Money*, Lee offered this biting summary: 'The promoters of *Hush Money* at His Majesty's Theatre would have been well advised to pay some of it in advance to the drama critic.'

One of Lee's more rewarding duties was to have a lasting effect on the rest of his life, although of course he could not have known it at the time. In 1911, at the age of 35, in his role as music critic, Lee reported on a

◁ Young Soloists. ▷

Miss GERTIE WILSON,
Soprano.

Miss DOROTHY BARRIE,
Contralto.

Joe Lee's sketches of the winners of a music competition in Dundee, made in 1910. Dorothy Barrie is top right.

Miss EVELYN WALKER,
Contralto.

Miss ADELAIDE MALCOLM,
Soprano

singing competition in which a 12-year-old girl, Dorothy Barrie, won the Gold Medal. Lee sketched the four finalists and published the drawings in the *City Echo*. Impressed by the young girl's talent, he kept in touch with her and took an interest in the development of her musical career. Dorothy Barrie was a talented violinist and pianist and within a couple of years of their meeting she left Dundee to study at the Royal Academy of Music in London. They would meet again.

Lee was much in demand as an artist at this time. He provided the illustrations for John Reid's publication *The Regality of Kirriemuir*, and contributed 28 pen drawings for *Lochee As It Was and As It Is* by Alexander Elliott in 1911. His collection of poems about Dundee, *Tales O' Our Town*, dedicated to his mother, was finally published in book form in 1910. Not only was it a fine collection of poems, but it also bore the very distinctive Lee trait of many fine pencil sketches to support the verse.

Lee's creative versatility at this time was astonishing. He turned his hand to play writing and in 1914 the students of the Dundee School of Art performed Lee's play *Fra Lippo Lippi*. Not an easy production, it comprised seven scenes featuring the career of the Italian painter, set of course in mediaeval times and mixing poetry and prose. Joseph Lee played the lead role, adding yet another string to his already fulsome bow.

Lee's work as a reporter, although at times mundane, did have occasional highs. The terrible Messina earthquake of 1908 was particularly relevant to him, as he had sailed through the Straits of Messina only a few years previously on his way to the Black Sea. More than half the population of Messina, 80,000 people, died in the disaster, which devastated an area that Lee's artistic eye had loved. His knowledge of the area was invaluable for the reporting of the event and it fell to him to compile the news feature.

In early 1912 a Yorkshireman, Linton Andrews, arrived at the *Dundee Advertiser* as

The cover of the programme for *Fra Lippo Lippi*, a play written by and starring Joseph Lee, which was performed in April 1914.

Souvenir Programme

Fra LIPPO LIPPI:

PAINTER, OF FLORENCE.

A PLAY IN   BY
SEVEN SCENES   JOSEPH LEE.

·FRA·LIPPO·LIPPI·

Performed by Students of the DUNDEE SCHOOL OF ART in the TECHNICAL COLLEGE on Wednesday and Thursday, 29th and 30th April, 1914.

assistant editor, on the princely wage of £5 per week. Andrews was to play a prominent part in Joe Lee's life. He recalls that Joe Lee was the music and art critic and had the 'head of a dark brooding Robbie Burns'. Robbie Burns was Lee's literary hero, so he would certainly have regarded that as a compliment! Andrews, in his *Autobiography of a Journalist*, provided an excellent insight into the workings of a newspaper office at that time. He comments that he was very quickly made aware, on taking up his appointment, that the editor, Alexander Urquhart, was not receptive to change. He was an excellent leader writer but had little interest in news or features. Within a few weeks, however, the newspaper would be faced with one of the major news features of the century, providing an opportunity for the new man Andrews to demonstrate his talents.

Joe Lee recalled vividly the reporting of the sinking of the *Titanic* on 14 April 1912 with the loss of 1,500 lives. Every staff member that could form a semi-colon was pressed into service. Amid clattering typewriters, endless scribbled notes, editorial meetings, urgent telephone calls and frenzied activity late into the night the newspaper team worked frantically in order to meet an impossible deadline. Impossible or not, the deadline was met. The news and resultant features ran into pages of print. Largely due to Andrews's organisational skills the newspaper produced an excellent publication and he was subsequently promoted by the newspaper's directors to take charge of news and features.

R.J.B. Sellar joined the staff of the *Dundee Advertiser* in 1910 and remembers the many talented people employed by the newspaper and its magazines in the period from 1910 to 1914. In particular he recalls Joe Lee in his role as editor of one of the local newspaper's magazines. By this time Lee was something of a local celebrity. Renowned for his drawings and his poems, and of course recognised as a local journalist, he was, as Sellars recalls, much admired by the younger staff. He didn't suffer fools gladly and would always argue a case with conviction. Like most talented, creative people he could be warm, good humoured and affable, but also brooding and occasionally feisty. He was, however, extremely popular with all his colleagues, who recognised and appreciated his *joie de vivre*. Above all he was an interesting man who commanded respect from his peers. His travels and range of interests had provided him with enviable experiences, which had enhanced his rich talents. Physically he was of medium height, stocky and powerfully built, with, as Sellars remembers, 'glowing, slumbering eyes'. Despite his local fame as poet, artist, playwright and journalist, Joseph Lee retained a modesty which endured throughout his life and endeared him to all those who knew him.

When Joe's mother Christina died in 1913 she had the satisfaction of knowing that her quiet, sensitive, asthmatic son, brought up in ghetto-like conditions, had become a much-respected figure. Sadly she did not live to see him married. The restless years of the first half of his life had left little time for romance. His travels abroad for lengthy unspecified periods and his forays to London, together with the blossoming of his many talents, made it extremely difficult to establish a long-lasting relationship. Nevertheless, he was enjoying the period of stability in his life, and his sister Kate had produced a daughter, Chrissie, making Joe a very proud uncle.

The editorial staff of John Leng & Co. were a close-knit bunch of hard-working journalists and reporters in those years just before the First World War. It was a winning combination of youth learning the ropes and experienced journalists who had been trained to cover everything from births, marriages, deaths and christenings to local competitions for the group's various newspapers and magazines. The *Dundee Advertiser*, *The People's Journal*, *The People's Friend* and the other publications were produced under the guidance of news editor Linton Andrews, and Joe Lee, now editor of *The People's Journal*. They were happy days for Joe Lee, requiring versatility, good humour and adaptability in order to meet the daily challenges. However, black clouds on the horizon heralded a storm which would engulf not only that happy team, but also the whole of Europe. Joe Lee would soon be torn away from his beloved Dundee and when he finally returned it would be to a saddened, shattered community.

CHAPTER THREE

Son of Dundee

THROUGHOUT his life Joe Lee would find himself, always, drawn back to Dundee. The town pulled at his emotions and drew him back to his roots. Exactly what he found irresistible about his home town is sometimes hard to understand. It is not as if he did not know better, or that he had little knowledge of the outside world. After all, as a young man, intelligent and well-read, his desire to experience alternatives to his existence had induced in him the desire to travel. At a time when travel was far from easy, indeed often arduous and dangerous, he had travelled extensively. He had crossed the Atlantic by cattle ship then progressed through the vast, wild plains of Canada; sailed through the Mediterranean to the exotic charms of Turkey and Russia; journeyed north to the Baltic Sea; experienced the more sophisticated European cities of Rotterdam, Amsterdam and Venice; and had lived in London and visited the city on several occasions before the First World War. Yet despite his exposure to the exotic, the sophisticated and the wilderness plains, he always returned to Dundee, a town once described as having a face 'only a mother could love'.

A more infamous description of Dundee came from the English writer Dr Samuel Johnson. Johnson, together with his biographer and Edinburgh lawyer James Boswell, toured the highlands of Scotland and the Hebrides in 1773. In his account of his travels, *Journey to the Western Islands of Scotland,* written in 1775, Johnson wrote 'crossed the Firth of Tay by ferry with the chaise; cost four shillings; stopped a while in Dundee where I remember nothing remarkable.' However in a letter to Hester Thrace he wrote 'We left St Andrews well satisfied with our reception crossing the Firth of Tay; came to Dundee, a dirty despicable town.' Dirty and despicable are harsh descriptions, but throughout its rich history Dundee has certainly had its moments.

Geographically, the setting of the town is one of the most spectacular in Britain. Nestling at the foot of two large hills, the Law and Balgay, the town spreads out up to and along the River Tay. On a clear day panoramic views from the top of the Law are breathtaking. Across the river Newport-on-Tay, linked to Dundee by a road bridge built in 1966 and the rail bridge built in 1878, which look like tiny Meccano models, sprawls eastwards towards Tayport, which nestles at the end of the peninsula. Tayport faces Broughty Ferry, a pleasant seaside town on the Dundee side of the Tay.

Looking towards the east, beyond Broughty Ferry and the Dundee docks can be seen the open sea, the North Sea, the lifeblood of Dundee. Carnoustie, world famous for its golf facilities, can just be glimpsed slightly to the north of Broughty Ferry, and turning further north across rolling meadow and farmland the Grampians stand out on a clear day. Turning westwards Joe Lee's much loved Sidlaw Hills dominate the

The view from the
Law over the River
Tay.

landscape and looking down on Balgay Hill the observatory can be seen on its tree-shrouded summit.

Dundee is well named, for its name gives to all Scots an immediate indication of its topography. 'Dun' is Gaelic for hill and 'daig' is believed to have been the name of an early tribal leader. It is no surprise to learn that early man found the area an ideal habitat. The hill named the Law offered a clear field of vision and was an ideal place to erect defences. Game was plentiful and the river, which is tidal, provided fresh water and an abundance of fish. Excavations have revealed burial mounds dating from 3500 BC, Iron Age remnants of wooden and stone defences, and Roman pottery, probably left from a first-century fort or look-out post. Evidence of even earlier residents was found when remains of woolly mammoths from the Ice Age were excavated.

However, it was the natural harbour that brought Dundee to prominence in the 12th century, and on the back of its growing reputation as a trading port it started to develop economically and politically. Its spreading influence made it a natural target in conflicts. From the 14th to the 17th century, many of history's prominent figures featured in the political struggles. Hollywood's *Braveheart*, William Wallace, was educated in Dundee. As good as any Hollywood script, the hot-tempered young Wallace, living in Dundee when it was captured and occupied by Edward I's forces, stabbed the son of an English nobleman during an argument and had to leave town in a hurry. Today a plaque in the High Street, near the site of the old Castle of Dundee, destroyed in 1314 and close to St Paul's Cathedral, indicates where the fight took place and states that it was here that Wallace struck the first blow for Scottish independence. Indeed Robert the Bruce was proclaimed King of Scots in Dundee in 1309, which sadly in later years ensured that Dundee would be a prominent port of call for successive English armies.

Edward I captured it, Henry VIII's army besieged and pounded it, the Duke of Montrose sacked it in 1645 and then, worst of all, in 1651 Dundee was caught up in the conflict of the English Civil War. Many Royalists, fleeing with their wealth, sought sanctuary in the town as General Monck, commanding Cromwell's army in Scotland, besieged it. At one stage in the battle, General Major Robert Lumsdaine, commanding Dundee's defence, retreated to the Old Steeple of St Mary's Tower for a last stand. When Monck called upon him to surrender he refused and indeed suggested in a polite letter that Monck himself should surrender and join him. Angered, Monck renewed his attack, and after 10 days Lumsdaine eventually surrendered. Lumsdaine was shot and beheaded; his head, mounted on a stake, was displayed on the pinnacle of the tower where it remained for several years. History does not tell us whether or not Monck ordered his execution, but he clearly was aware of the humiliation heaped on Lumsdaine by the display of his head and may well have turned a blind eye to his execution. It would seem that the wealthy Royalists, seeking sanctuary in Dundee with their gold coins and silverware, sealed the town's fate as the victors quickly snapped up the booty.

Joe Lee, in a long narrative poem from his book *Tales O' Our Town* called 'The Storming of The Old Steeple', movingly describes this event in Dundee's history. An extract graphically demonstrates the injustice that Lee feels the townspeople suffered:

> This is the tale:–
>   Cromwell and Charles
> Are fighting out their bloody quarrels,
> And Monck is left, with mighty hand
> To pacify, or plague Scotland,
> In the old way we know so well –
> With mine and mortar, shot and shell –
> To bring the troublous towns to reason –
> For what is loyalty in season,
> A day or two may turn to treason;

Later verses go on to say:

> No records show what deeds were done
> Under that old September sun;
> We know that blood in rivers ran,
> That once again man murdered man
> As ah! how oft since Cain began.

He tells of the fate of Lumsdaine:

> And so heroic hearts did not avail,
> And so comes to an end the sad old tale –
> A noble head struck on an iron nail.

This sacking of Dundee was ruthless and thorough and when the town was attacked again, just before the Battle of Killiecrankie in 1689, by Viscount Dundee, its destruction was almost complete.

The Mercat Cross, now in Nethergate. It dates from 1586 and was formerly situated in Seagate. The cross is the subject of two of Lee's poems about Dundee.

A particularly black period in the town's history is featured in *Tales O'Our Town* when Lee writes of the last witch burning in Dundee at the Mercat Cross in Seagate, in November 1669. The story is particularly poignant and gruesome. The 'witch', Grizzel Jaffray, had a son, a master mariner, whose ship returned to Dundee on the very day that his mother was being burned. It is believed that he saw the flames and asked a passer-by what was happening. When he discovered the truth it is said that he set sail again immediately, never to return to Dundee. Lee writes in his poem 'Grizzel Jaffray':

> They have taen her to the Witches' Pool
> To see if she would droon;
> And the waters went not ower her head,
> But the current bare her roun'.

> 'If my stout son had been at hame,
> As he is on the sea,
> The bauldest men amang ye a'
> Had not put this shame on me.'

They have taen her to the Mercat Cross,
    To see if she would burn
And ere the flames came ower her head
    A ship she did discern.

'If that were but my son's stout ship,
    As it is on the sea
There's nane the bravest o' them a',
    Dare have put this death on me.'

When the son discovers the truth he says:

'O, mither, had I been at hame,
    As I was on the sea
There's nane the bravest o' them a'
Had lain this death on thee.

'How often from the cauld and heat,
    Hast thou been shield to me,
And yet from these same cruel fires
    I might not succour thee!

Dundee was a sad and despicable town indeed! In those times witch burning was not the sole preserve of Dundonians and was a common occurrence throughout Britain. By the time Samuel Johnson visited Dundee in 1773, despite his assertions about the town, it was slowly recovering from its ravages, fuelled largely by sea trade. The process of recovery was aided by a quirk of fate which launched the first of the three J's so synonymous with Dundee's later commercial and industrial success. 'Jam, jute and journalism' were the three J's; supported by ship building and whaling.

Popular folklore tells how marmalade was invented in Dundee. In 1797 a cargo ship, battered by heavy storms, was forced into Dundee harbour. The captain, in order to cut his losses, decided to sell the cargo and a local grocer, James Keiller, bought a large consignment of oranges. However, when his wife closely examined his purchase she found that most of the fruit had turned sour. Determined to salvage what she could from a poor investment she boiled the oranges with sugar, creating a delicious orange jam. Of course, there are many explanations and stories about how and where marmalade was invented, including perhaps the most famous, which attributes it to a preparation made for a poorly Mary Queen of Scots: the name is said to be a contraction of the phrase 'Marie malade', meaning that the Queen was unwell. Whatever the truth of the matter, Keiller's became a successful producer of marmalade and jam.

Factories started producing and selling the product throughout Britain, but 'Dundee could not live on jam alone'. Commercial whaling had also begun to prosper, with whale oil a vital source of energy. The increasing number of boats and intense competition sometimes meant that fleets would venture as far as the Arctic in search of their prey. It was a hard, cold, dangerous industry, but helped to bring prosperity to the town.

By the early 1800s Scots living in Calcutta recognised that Dundee, with its good harbour, accessible sea route, whale oil and labour force would be an ideal base for the importation and processing of jute. Their reasoning was sound, and they started exporting jute to Dundee in vast quantities for processing. For more than a hundred years the jute industry would sustain the economy of Dundee, indeed creating boom town conditions. Mills and textile factories processing the imported raw material into bags and carpet backing sprang up all over Dundee. Attracted by the prospect of employment, workers flooded into the area. Catholic Highlanders and many Irish, fleeing from their devastating potato famine, brought a volatile mix into an already complex cocktail of humanity. Tough fishermen, hardened whalers returning from difficult and dangerous voyages, did not always take kindly to the influx of foreigners invading their favourite drinking haunts, chatting up their women and literally invading their space. Fist fights, flashing knives and angry voices were a nightly occurrence in the many bars along the waterfront. Accommodation was a real problem, and as more and more workers flocked to the town, they were crammed into overcrowded tenements. Several workers would share a room and whole families would be squeezed into just two rooms.

In *Tales O' Our Town* Joe Lee includes his translation of a poem originally by the German poet Heinrich Heine, which movingly tells of the day-to-day struggle of the weavers. He notes at the end of the poem that at its first appearance it was suppressed by the censors. The final verse reads:

'The great looms groan, and the shuttles flee,
Day and night we are weaving unceasingly;
Our country, we weave for thee now a shroud,
With a threefold curse for the haughty and proud –
We weave, we weave!'

There is another poem about the weavers, called 'Lays of the Loom', which is Joe Lee's own. It begins:

The whistles' loud weary wailing
Is calling me from my bed,
Like the shrill Last Trumpet calling
The sinfu', unwilling dead

From the shelter of my poor room,
To the cheerless streets and chill
I go, for my doom is the living tomb
Of the great gaunt grimy mill

One verse grimly tells of a spinner leaving her loom to endure a stillbirth, vividly demonstrating the scant regard for human life.

Here I toiled till the day I bore him,
Till I fell on the sacks in a swound;
Here I toiled till from me they tore him,
And hid him away in the ground.

The struggle for survival in the North Sea and the Arctic was just as hard for the whalers, and sometimes, despite risking life and limb, the ships would return empty and catchless, and that meant no wages with which to feed their families, a situation that Lee describes in his poem 'The Whalers', which is subtitled 'A chanty of home-coming'.

> Our batter'd, broken bows borne back
>   By the cruel ice, and keen,
> We could not make the Nor' Wat-er
>   An' we're so returnin' – 'clean'.
> An' fat years, by-gone, o' oil an' bone
>   Wi' men nor masters don't atone
> For a year that is lank and lean.

So although this period was regarded as prosperous, for some it certainly was not. The early morning whistles would summon thousands of workers stumbling into the cold streets – icy streets in the winter – where they would move in huge groups to the factory or mill. All day, late into the night, the massive wheels would noisily whirl and the shuttles would fly. Chimneys, from mill and factory, spewed smoke, which billowed into the sky creating a hazy fog over the whole area that was poisonous to lungs. Kathleen Blackwood remembers as a young girl climbing Law Hill and not being able to see the town for smoke. Dundee was an industrial working-class city with all the problems brought about by boom without control. At one time almost 50,000 people were employed in more than 75 jute mills, with several thousand more employed in the jam factories, all of which poured smoke and pollution into the sky.

The image, certainly familiar from Victorian times, of hard pressed working-class people toiling all hours for a pittance is well captured by Lee. But as always, of course, there is the other side of the equation. The jute industry made millionaires of a number of people and their grand houses, built in the seaside resort of Broughty Ferry four miles from Dundee, bear ample testimony to their success. A number of entrepreneurs built on their success in the jute industry to finance other projects, notably in America. Texas in particular benefited from Scottish investment in cattle and oil. Incredibly the massive Texas oil industry owes its success to funding originating from Dundee's jute industry.

All good things, however, do come to an end. India eventually started to develop its own processing capability and imports of raw jute began to dwindle. The boom had lasted more than 100 years, and in the 1950s there were still more than 7,000 people employed in the business. Today it is all but dead, but its heritage is kept alive at the Verdant Works, a former jute mill where the history of jute processing is commemorated in an award-winning museum. Jam making too has diminished, having reached its peak, perhaps, in the 1950s. It has suffered from the vast increase in consumer choice and by the mid-1980s the industry in Dundee was in terminal decline.

However the third 'J', journalism, is thriving. D.C. Thomson, whose present-day company was founded in 1905, is located in an impressive sandstone building in Albert Square and is one of Britain's largest publishers, producing more than 200 million periodicals, magazines, comics and newspapers each year, which are distributed all over Britain. Its impressive growth has led to offices being established in Manchester, Glasgow and London, where it is the largest national publisher in Fleet Street. Since its founding in 1905 the company has been responsible for

D.C. Thomson and Co., Albert Square, Dundee. The company was founded in 1905.

producing well over 100 comics and magazines, including most of Britain's favourites such as the *Dandy* and the *Beano*. This family-run business, which has diversified into television and the Internet, has been a constant factor in the economic success of Dundee, employing more than 1,700 people locally.

In 1905 Dundee had another well-established publishing company, John Leng & Co., which operated out of Bank Street, where Joe Lee became the editor of *The People's Journal*. The contribution of these two excellent companies to Dundee's history is huge.

Jute, jam and whaling brought further industry to Dundee: shipbuilding. Cargo ships were constantly in demand, as were new commercial whaling ships as the fleets expanded. Shipbuilding was a natural by-product of the success in other areas. The demand for new ships and repairs to old enhanced the town's maritime reputation.

Whale oil, once very much in demand, became scarce as whale stocks started to diminish. Over-fishing eventually killed off the whaling industry in Dundee, but shipbuilding continued.

Dundee's reputation, particularly for building wooden ships, earned it the contract from the Royal Geographical Society to build a scientific research ship capable of withstanding the impact of crushing ice floes. The vessel, which was to spend two winters in the Antarctic, was built and launched on the Tay in 1901 and would be forever enshrined in Britain's maritime history as Captain Scott's *Discovery*. However, another ship, the *Terra Nova*, also Dundee-built, carried Scott to the South Pole for his fatal failed odyssey in 1911. Pleasingly the Maritime Trust purchased the *Discovery* in 1986 and returned her to Dundee, where she is on display at Discovery Point, moored in a specially allocated quay.

As the history of Dundee unfolds, one can see why Lee fell in love with his home town, but there are also reasons why one might want to get away from such a place. During Lee's childhood and early teens, there were a number of notable landmarks in the town's development. Dundee University was founded in 1883; Queen Victoria granted the town a Charter in 1889; and the Tay rail bridge was finally repaired in 1887. At the time of its construction in 1878 the bridge, at over two miles long, was the longest in Europe and was a much-needed, long-awaited, link over the Tay. Tragically, on a bitterly cold night on 28 December 1879, a section of the bridge collapsed as a train approached. It fell into the Tay, killing 90 passengers and crew. Lee did not feature any of these events in his poems of Dundee, perhaps because he was only a small boy at the time of the disaster, and he would not live to see the construction of the Tay road bridge, which was completed in 1966.

At the beginning of the 20th century, one of the country's leading figures focussed the national spotlight on Dundee. From 1908–22 the town had the distinction of being represented in Parliament by one of the great figures of British history and arguably the greatest political leader in the history of these islands. A very young Winston Churchill was appointed a Cabinet Minister by Prime Minister Herbert Asquith, who needed to find him a constituency. His first attempt standing as a Liberal in north-west Manchester was unsuccessful, but on his third attempt, standing in Dundee, he was elected. That same year, 1908, he married Clementine, and although the marriage was a success his early political career was controversial. Given Dundee's uncompromising and often tough and violent history, Churchill, paradoxically born into luxury at Blenheim Palace, with a privileged lifestyle and accent to match, appeared to have the tough characteristics that Dundonians respected and admired. It was well documented that he had fought hand-to-hand against the dervishes at Omdurman in 1898 with the 21st Lancers and during the Boer War he had seen action, had been taken prisoner and later escaped. Later, during the First World War, despite holding high office and being in a position to avoid active service, he went to France as a Major in the Oxfordshire Hussars and later commanded the 6th Battalion Royal Scots Fusiliers.

Churchill had guts, was outspoken and certainly gave Dundee a high profile in British politics. In 1910 he became Home Secretary, was made First Lord of the Admiralty in 1911 and became Minister of Munitions and Air in 1917. Sadly, although he was given great credit for preparing the British fleet for war, the disaster in the Dardanelles, when Britain sustained over 200,000 casualties, was blamed unfairly on him. It was said that the disaster stayed with him for the rest of his life.

Churchill, during his time as a politician, tried to improve workers' conditions in factories and workshops but in 1922 the Conservatives forced Prime Minister Lloyd George to resign, necessitating a general election. In the early stages of the campaign Churchill was taken ill with appendicitis and was unable to travel up to Dundee to campaign. Clementine, his wife, decided that as he had to be represented she would start the campaign for him. She kept him up to date with progress reports, advising him that the newspaper comments were vile; there was misery everywhere and some of the people appeared to be starving. Certainly there had been a change of heart about Churchill in Dundee; many Dundonians disliked what they perceived as his warmongering and the campaign was difficult, with Clementine being shouted down at meetings and on occasions spat upon. Despite this behaviour she did say that although the people could be abusive, they were on the whole good-natured.

Churchill did eventually manage to put in an appearance in Dundee, but despite making several brilliant speeches, he lost the election having served Dundee for 14 years. It is believed that Churchill never forgave Dundee for rejecting him at the polls and preferring local man Ned Scrymgeour. Churchill wrote, many years later, that he found himself in 1923 in the political wilderness 'without an office, without a seat, without a party and without an appendix.' This blip in his fortunes, as history tells us, was momentary, and of course he went on to become the greatest leader of modern times. Dundee can claim that it gave him the opportunity to foster and nurture his skills and prepared him for the greatness to come. Certainly during his time in Dundee he had both reached the heights and plumbed the depths – invaluable experience indeed!

Interestingly, the Lee family became connected to the Scrymgeours through marriage. Joe Lee's younger sister Kate's first daughter, Chrissie Blackwood, married James Thomson Scrymgeour in Dundee on 27 January 1940. He was a nephew of Dundee's MP, Ned. So, uniquely, Mrs Nancy Hughes of Tayport is the great-niece of Ned Scrymgeour and the great-niece of Joe Lee, two men who both contributed enormously to the history of the town.

* * * * *

The painful development of Dundee, battered by history and its people exploited and abused by industry, is featured in Joseph Lee's first book of poems, *Tales O'Our Town*, published in 1910. Many of the town's historic events, characters, buildings and streets are described, accompanied by fine pen and pencil sketches. The suffering of the people is accurately and meaningfully portrayed as Lee records the hardship and struggle of the working class: the whalers, the fishermen, the weavers and the factory workers. Despite being an experienced journalist, he never wrote about his feelings, especially about the exploitation of the people, other than through his poetry. Later on in his life, during the war years, he would again use the same vehicle to express his emotions. He never recorded his wartime experiences save through his eyes as artist and poet. Lee's decision to translate and include Heine's poem 'The Weavers' in his book suggests he sympathised with the German poet's view, which rails against the harsh conditions of the weavers cursing God and the King of the rich:

> 'A curse on the God unto whom we cried,
> When our people perished for lack of bread;
> In vain did we hope, and in vain did we wait,
> He fooled and derided, and mocked at our fate.
>> We weave, we weave!
>
> A curse on the King – of the rich – for he
> Has not sought to soften our misery,
> But from us has wrung the last farthing we'd got,
> Then left us like dogs in the street to be shot.
>> We weave, we weave!

Joe Lee's own large family lived in cramped, inadequate rooms in one of the tenements. The accommodation created its own pressures, exacerbated by the daily struggle for survival. Lee experienced at first-hand the frustration boiling over into arguments, not only within his own family but also within the neighbourhood, as the people grew weary of the daily grind. Kathleen Blackwood recalled that her mother Kate, Joe's favourite younger sister, remembered her early working days. Although she was only 13 at the time she started work, she worked long hours and during the winter nights would have to return home in darkness. The tenement was in Wellgate, a seedy, squalid part of the town, at the top of the building, accessed by a long, winding stone stairway. The stairway was lit by guttering gas mantles set at intervals, but often the mantles had been allowed to go out. Progress up the stairway in total darkness was precarious and made worse by the occasional prostrate body of a drunk, garnished by vomit and worse. Muggers and drunks and fighting neighbours formed part of the obstacle course for a frightened 13-year-old girl.

Yet despite the squalor of some parts of the town, many of Lee's poems at this time were of places in the town which he particularly loved. The old Mercat Cross featured in the poem about the burning of the witch Grizzel Jaffray, and was also the subject of its own poem, 'The Auld Mercat Cross'. The poem records an extraordinary encounter with pirates on the seas:

> Of Captain Crichton an' the Pirate
> I' the East Indies, somewhat irate,
> Till tauld o' auld Cross o' Dundee,
> Whan; 'We be townsmen, thee an' me,
> Set skipper, ship, an' cargo free!'

In the footnote to the poem Joe Lee gives the story of Captain Crichton, of Dundee, who with his ship was captured in 1750 by Angria, a notorious pirate of the East Indies. Angria asked Crichton where he originally came from. When Crichton said Dundee, Angria asked him where the cross of Dundee stood. Crichton answered 'Near the west end of the large square, opposite the new Townhouse.' Angria appeared satisfied and then asked him how many steps it had. Crichton responded, 'Six steps all round it.' Angria replied, 'Quite right. Well Captain Crichton, because we are townsmen I give you your liberty and your ship in a present.'

Joe Lee's own sketch of the Mercat Cross.

Lee told the tale of Lumsdaine's last stand in 'The Storming of the Old Steeple', but also wrote a poem about St Mary's Tower itself, entitled 'St Mary's: The Old Steeple'. The tower is now the oldest surviving building in Dundee. However, the present edifice is only a fraction of what was once a superb mediaeval church, the largest in Scotland. It was built in 1192 by the brother of King William the Lion of Scotland David, Earl of Huntingdon, was returning from the Third Crusade when his ship got caught in severe storms. When disaster seemed inevitable he prayed for deliverance, vowing to build a church in gratitude if he should survive. Survive he did, and he kept his word. Over the centuries the church has been attacked on several occasions but despite all assaults it has survived, although parts have been lost and additions made.

Lee writes about the traffic and tumult of the town rolling round the feet of the tower, and notes how it gazes down upon the streets. It is a landmark for sailors, its weather-beaten walls are pockmarked from General Monck's musket fire and of course he remembers those who died defending the building.

Although much of Lee's verse concerned historical events and at times could be morose and moving, he did have a light, whimsical, almost satirical poetic voice when required. He had a great love and respect for the Scots poet Robert Burns, whose works clearly inspired him. One day while walking through Albert Square in Dundee he spotted three workmen cleaning the statue of Burns, using brushes, mops, soda and soap. Inspired by the sight he wrote a very long poem called 'The White-Washin' O' Robbie Burns', in which he discusses the indignity with Robbie Burns himself. Witty and amusing, it received great acclaim when published in *The People's Journal*.

Another famous Dundee landmark that inspired Lee's pen is the Howff. Near the D.C. Thomson building in Albert Square, it is a burial ground, granted to Dundee in 1565 by Mary Queen of Scots. Lee's poem is tongue-in-cheek, with some irreverent lines:

> Vast meeting place where all are mute
> For dust has ended the dispute

Although today it is an old cemetery, the Howff was once the site of a
Franciscan monks' church, where in the 14th century the clergy
recognised Robert the Bruce as King. In the 16th century the area formed
part of the city's defences. Today it stands silent and untroubled, an

The White-Washin'
o' Robbie Burns –
Joe Lee's
illustration to
accompany his
poem.

amazing time capsule of history, social change and human tragedy, with
people's names engraved lovingly on tombstones which betray their age as
they deteriorate. Many of the old gravestones carry the marks of the old
trades and crafts guilds: weavers, shoemakers, bakers, skinners, dyers,
butchers, tailors, glovers and hammermen.

The hammermen represented skilled craftsmen like goldsmiths, silversmiths, pewter men, gun makers, locksmiths and buckle makers. Other trades, including masons, wrights, slaters, cabinetmakers and tinsmiths are also commemorated. The gravestones also bear testimony to the harshness of the times with dozens recording the deaths of infants and teenagers. It would seem that very few families escaped the tragedy of an early death in the family.

Some gravestones offer a more exotic glimpse of the past, recording the demise of shipmasters, sea captains and sailors, while one commemorates the death of a lieutenant of the French Imperial Guard. Jules Legendre, who was born in France in 1785 and fought for his country, later settled in Dundee, where he married a local girl and died in 1840. The cemetery also contains a more modern burial, housing the grave of James Chalmers, the local man who gave Britain, and the world, the adhesive postage stamp.

Lee's poem about the Howff is light and satirical, and one can picture him sitting among the gravestones quietly composing while the residents are quietly decomposing.

Lee loved the open air, loved to walk free and loved to feel the wind on his face. His poetry sums up his feelings, particularly about the landscape around Dundee. His poem about the Sidlaw Hills, inspired by a bout of homesickness while in Canada, was followed by poems dedicated to the Law and Balgay Hill. In the poem about the Law, a mischievous couplet indicates that it wasn't just for the fresh air that the locals visited the hill:

> Fair trystin'-place for lad an' lass,
> Nae notice boards 'keep aff the grass!'

The poem about Balgay Hill intriguingly tells the story of a jilted lass. Did Lee know the lassie? Did he do the jilting? At this time in his life there is no record of a steady relationship, although some of his poetry hints at romance, although that is, after all, a favourite subject for many poets. Whether the poem was written from experience or from imagination, it is a sad story of unrequited love.

On Balgay Hill there grows the beech,
    On Balgay Hill there grows the birk,
Whare me and my luve wont to meet
    Betwixt the gloamin' and the mirk.

The poem concludes:

O, foolish love sae quick to go,
    O, foolish heart sae quick to twine;
Had I but known what now I know,
    He ne'er had gotten love o' mine.

O, foolish heart sae quick to trust,
    O, wilful will sae quick to bend,
Would that my head were happ'd in dust,
    And a' my cares were at an end.

It was on Balgay Hill that Lee just missed meeting Rudyard Kipling, who had visited the observatory and left just before Lee arrived.

One of the main streets of Dundee, Nethergate, had a distinctive fascination for Lee. In a poem called 'The Nethergate', dedicated 'To all who have wandered forth from our ancient city by any of its many gates', he actually notes that despite his travels and experiences it is Dundee, and Nethergate in particular, which has his affection:

Frae wand'ring up and down the earth
I've sought the city of my birth,
And marked it still the same to-day
As I had never been away,
    And found it Home – and blessed my fate,
That set me in the Nethergate.

Quite how Lee would regard modern Dundee is open to conjecture. The numerous mills are silent, no shrieking whistles summon the workers to another day of hardship, no smoke shrouds the skies, no whaling fleets

The Howff cemetery, Dundee. The burial ground was given to the people of Dundee by Mary Queen of Scots in 1565.

lie at anchor and there is no industrial base. Dundee is, however, a modern, thriving vibrant city, the fourth largest in Scotland. Its natural harbour is still an invaluable asset and it has developed light engineering, electronics, textiles, and education research, and it has enhanced its newspaper-publishing base to help maintain its economic prosperity. Yet sadly much of what Lee wrote about has gone. Much of the mediaeval part of the town was destroyed in town planning disasters from 1962 to the late 1970s. Later attempts to promote more tasteful development have been more successful, although the ultra-modern Overgate shopping centre, with its huge glass front, directly confronts St Mary's Tower. The Wellgate area that was home to the Lee family, squalid though it was, has been destroyed and the site is now the Wellgate multi-storey car park.

The Mercat Cross of carved stone dates back to 1586 and at the time of the burning of Grizzel Jaffray the witch in 1669 it was situated in Seagate. In 1750, at the time of the encounter between Captain Crichton and Angria the pirate, Crichton confirmed that the Dundee Cross had six steps all round it. However, during Lee's time in 1874 the cross was moved to its present position in Nethergate, close to St Mary's Tower and in view of the Overgate Centre. The only change to the cross itself since Lee's time has been the addition of a bronze unicorn to the top of the shaft in the 1960s. St Mary's Tower, the Howff burial ground, the Robbie Burns statue in Albert Square and the offices of D.C. Thomson are all very much as they were. From a distance Lee's old offices at Bank Street, where he edited *The People's Journal* for John Leng & Co., look relatively unchanged. Indeed the façade of the magnificent row of Victorian sandstone buildings still carries the legend, in large capital letters, 'DUNDEE AD-VERTISER, EVENING TELEGRAPH, PEOPLE'S FRIEND and PEOPLE'S JOURNAL'. The entrance to the office still exists, but sadly the hustle and bustle and the happy camaraderie of a busy newspaper publishing operation has gone. The superb street still retains its character, but the buildings have been filled by flats, a hairdressers, a beauty salon, a restaurant, a bridal gown shop and other retail outlets.

The former offices of Thomson-Leng on Bank Street, where Joe Lee worked as editor of *The People's Journal*.

Joe Lee would recognise and approve the Verdant Works, preserved as a museum and, Joe would likely feel, a tribute to the suffering of the people. Dundee still has some impressive buildings and streets of character, such as the excellent Victorian sandstone buildings of Commercial Street, Whitehall Street and the Crescent, and of course, despite changes, Joe Lee's beloved Nethergate. The city retains, albeit in a different form, the original main streets or gates: Corngate, Seagate, Marketgate and Overgate.

Some things of course never change, and Joe Lee would certainly

The war memorial
on the Law
overlooking
Dundee that
commemorates the
dead of the Battle
of Loos, 1915.

recognise the icy, wintry wind blasting from the Tay through the narrow streets and onto Nethergate and High Street.

However, it is the view from the top of the Law that would be the greatest change. Lee would be familiar with the impressive monument dedicated to the fallen at Loos in the First World War in 1915, built on top of the 570ft summit. The monument has at its peak a beacon that is lit on special occasions, but always on 25 September to commemorate the Battle of Loos. The views from the top of the Law are still as spectacular as they ever were, but there are marked differences now that the town has been freed from the industrial smoke and fog which spewed from the jute mills and textile factories. Lee wryly commented in his poem 'The Law', after praising the magnificent views:

> A host o' distant things ye'll see –
> Of course ye'll no look for Dundee
> 'Mang it's smoke an' a';

Certainly the mills are silent now, and just one large chimney-stack stands out on the horizon as a monument to the past. Although many of the old factories and mills have been converted into flats and apartments, Dundee has sprawled towards the slopes of the Law and Balgay Hill; much of the open grassland and wooded lower reaches, once seen as an escape from the grim, dirty town has gone as development has spread further and higher. Lee would be aggrieved by this, as he surely would be by the sight of several tall, characterless, modern apartment blocks spoiling the view towards the Tay. He would certainly approve of the Tay road bridge, opened in 1966 and one of the longest road bridges in Britain at one and a half miles long, and be delighted by the development of the Mills Observatory on Balgay. This public observatory gives everyone a unique opportunity to observe the universe. Lee, with his inquisitive, romantic mind, would embrace the exploration of the heavens. He would also approve of the way in which Dundee, over the past few years, has actively nurtured and developed its arts community. There has been a real effort made to appreciate and preserve the city's historical and cultural heritage. Verdant Works is one example, while the McManus Galleries in Albert Square detail the history, with supporting exhibits, of the city from the Iron Age up to today. The Victorian Gallery, inside the Albert Hall, has a very fine range of paintings from Dutch, French, British and particularly Scottish artists.

One of Joe Lee's major interests was of course drama, and he would be delighted by the fact that theatre is very much alive in modern Dundee. Dundee Contemporary Arts in Nethergate provides the city with the latest arthouse productions as well as a platform for a variety of exhibitions, visual research facilities and a print studio.

Live theatre is catered for by the Repertory Theatre with its resident company of 14 actors, which provides the venue not only for local productions, but also for national touring productions as well. Caird Hall in the City Square is the venue for concerts and has a varied programme throughout the year and together with the Whitehall Theatre caters for virtually all tastes. Lee would be quite at home reviewing the latest play or musical production for his old employer John Leng, although at the time of the First World War they were under the umbrella of D.C. Thomson, which is still a major part of Dundee's community. Dundee has of course moved on for its part. Its harshest critics would say perhaps not far! Certainly until more recent times it had been less than sensitive in preserving and enhancing its heritage, yet the Dundee that Lee revered was far from beautiful.

The wildness and spectacular topography of the city is beyond question, but also, as well as his raw emotion at the exploitation of the workers and his observations of the poverty and hardship of his time, Lee had a genuine love for the people and the city. Nostalgia certainly played its part and often time softens an experience and the luxury of reflection can change its perspective.

Lee's poem 'The Old School' in *Tales O' Our Town* is an example. It is sharply observational, poignant and nostalgic, as he revisits his old school, recalling fellow pupils and the cricket captain, who later drowned in the Magellan Sea.

> I wander on as in a dream;
> The things which I was wont to deem
> So wondrous large – how small they seem!

He continues:

> I hear the swishing sweep of cane;
> A fly hums on the window pane –
> Lo! I am a schoolboy once again!

The poem ends:

> Even so our lives do slip away;
> A little while of work and play –
> A longer or a shorter stay –
>
> And then Death opens wide the door;
> The school's dismissed, the tasks are o'er,
> We go, and we return no more.

The 18 three-line verses of reminiscence recognise that life, like school, is a learning process which eventually comes full circle. It is a beautiful piece of writing.

Despite his love and fascination for his hometown no one could claim that Lee made his observations through rose-tinted spectacles, far from it. In fact one could see that he was, on occasions, apt to view darkly.

* * * * *

Dundee has a rich heritage marked by conquest and strife, momentous events and figures to grace any historic Hall of Fame. Wallace started the fire, Robert the Bruce picked up the gauntlet and yet it was a Dundee man, Admiral Duncan, who saved Britain from invasion in 1797. Duncan, born in 1731, defeated the Dutch fleet at Camperdown, preventing a planned invasion of Britain by France and Holland. It was Duncan's shrewd tactics that carried the day, and he was awarded estates now called Camperdown Country Park, which today are open to the public, and he was made a peer of the realm as a reward for his brilliance. There is also a very impressive statue of him located opposite the William Wallace plaque near St Paul's Cathedral.

Other notable Dundee contributions to Britain are the building of the *Discovery*, the invention of the adhesive postage stamp by James Chalmers and the development of the young Winston Churchill. The town has also famously given Britain, and the world, marmalade, Dundee cake and a whole range of reading habits from the *Dandy* and *Beano* to a plethora of publications that are now widely read in British households.

Less impressively, perhaps, the city ejected its Member of Parliament, Winston Churchill, who went on to become Sir Winston Churchill, the greatest political leader of the 20th century.

It is my contention, however, that Dundee also gave Britain one of the finest of all First World War poets: Sergeant Joe Lee, the Black Watch poet. As the clouds of war gathered across Europe in early 1914, Joe Lee, immersed in his work on *The People's Journal* and his many cultural interests, with a published book of poems about his beloved Dundee to his name, can have had little inkling of what lay ahead.

CHAPTER FOUR

Fighter Writer

B Y THE spring of 1914 it was becoming increasingly obvious that Germany's ambitions for territorial expansion could only result in war. Months of frenzied diplomatic activity throughout the capitals of Europe had done little to dampen Germany's ambition. It was wary of the Triple Entente of Britain, France and Russia and could only rely on Austria-Hungary as an ally, following Britain's rejection of its attempts at an alliance. The spark to trigger war came with the assassination, in Sarajevo in June 1914, of Archduke Franz Ferdinand, the heir to the Austro-Hungarian throne. The murder was believed to have been instigated by a Serbian political organisation and provided the excuse for Austria and Hungary, supported by Germany, to declare war on Serbia. All attempts at rapprochement on all sides rapidly disappeared, and the dominoes of war in Europe started to fall over.

Germany declared war on Russia and then France and, when the Germans invaded neutral Belgium on 4 August 1914, Britain declared war on Germany. More dominoes started to fall when Montenegro declared war on Austria, Serbia on Germany, Austria on Russia and finally Britain and France declared war on Austria. Prior to the formal declaration of hostilities, the newspapers in Britain had not been optimistic about avoiding conflict and many people regarded war, especially given Germany's attitude, as inevitable. There was, however, an article in the *Daily Mail*, which conveyed complacency but also provoked outrage in many quarters. The newspaper suggested that Britain could rely on its well-trained Indian army to match the Germans. For many red-blooded young Britons the suggestion that native troops should do the fighting for them was an insult. In addition, German boasts that the Fatherland would one day rule the world only helped to fan the flames of resentment.

The publishing houses of John Leng & Co. and D.C. Thomson in Dundee probably typified the spirit of the time. Groups of young men working together formed a common bond, a resolution to resist the enemy. 'The Germans have been asking for it and now they're going to get it' perhaps best summarised the mood. The young lions of the British Empire were stirring as they smelled a fight.

In Dundee the legendary Black Watch started to mobilise volunteer Territorials to form a 4th Battalion, while the neighbouring town of Angus and local fishing villages recruited a 5th Battalion. Perthshire and Fife supplied further battalions. Most of the young editorial staff of Leng's and Thomson's left their jobs and enlisted. Young, impatient and wanting to fight they did not want to join the Territorials, fearing that they would see little action, preferring to join the Black Watch regulars. However, many found that, having signed the recruitment forms, they had indeed enlisted in the Territorials. Understandably, given the history and the glamour of the Black Watch, they envisaged themselves fighting gloriously in the black and blue tartan kilt and red hackle. In the very early days of recruitment journalists and other employed applicants were sometimes rejected as recruits. Preference was given to the unemployed and the destitute and down-and-out. Very soon, however, full mobilisation removed that doubtful qualification.

Joe Lee did not volunteer immediately and of course, being almost 40 years old with bronchial asthma, nobody expected him to. However, the office must quickly have become a lonely place. A colleague, R.J.B. Sellar, recalls that one day he was on duty at the Drill Hall, Bank Street, Dundee, when Joe Lee walked in and announced that he wanted to join the army. When Sellar asked him how old he was, Joe told him to mind his own business and said 'just give me my kilt'. It is suggested that Joe was less than accurate when stating his age on the recruitment form.

In those early days the cramped, crowded Drill Hall, home to the new recruits, was a far from comfortable place. The uneducated, formerly unemployed recruits were not terribly worried about social or hygiene

Joe Lee resplendent
in the uniform of
the Black Watch.

standards. Soon the barrack room became dirty, smelly and noisy. Arguments, drunkenness, vomiting, smoking, thieving and prostitution were not to the liking of the few professional men who had managed to enlist. In addition to the diabolical living conditions, extreme frustration resulted from a lack of uniforms and rifles. The system had been unable to cope; caught unawares by the huge, unexpected influx of volunteers from the jute mills and jam factories. Gradually conditions improved as more professional men enlisted and indeed a considerable group of journalists, writers and artists, including Joe Lee and Linton Andrews, started to accumulate. They called themselves the 'Fighter Writers.'

Linton Andrews, a Yorkshireman, was the odd man out since all the others were Scottish, and to illustrate the paranoia of the time, because of his English accent and his ability to read foreign newspapers, he was regarded with suspicion. Reacting to rumours that he might be a spy, an officer, Captain Boase, called him in for questioning. Despite being the news editor of the *Dundee Advertiser*, Andrews had to obtain character references. Later in the war, however, Andrews would prove to Captain Boase, beyond any doubt, where his loyalties lay.

Weapons and uniforms duly arrived and a period of intense training followed, with domestic duties allocated to the Territorial Battalion while they were billeted in a variety of local residences. Periods of drilling, to instill discipline and order, helped to bond the units, while patrolling and guarding local power and communications points gave them a sense of purpose. Cold winter nights patrolling the Tay Bridge, guarding Broughty Ferry, protecting the town's water supply and submarine dry dock and undergoing weapons training, gave the men a taste of what was to come. The Fighter Writers found it particularly hard to adjust to army orders and discipline in the early stages. Well educated, opinionated, able to respond quickly to deadlines and used to acting on initiative, it was difficult for them to suppress the view that they, perhaps, could run the army more efficiently. Firm officers quickly persuaded them of the error of their ways and training continued until at last they were considered proficient enough for service.

The 4th Battalion of the Black Watch, 'Dundee's Own', 900 strong, consisted of fathers, sons, uncles, brothers, cousins, nephews and work mates and on 23 February 1915 they departed for France from Dundee railway station. Massive crowds of tearful mothers and girlfriends, and proud fathers, watched as the men marched and sang, accompanied by the skirl of the pipes, as they made their way to the station. This was what it was all about: camaraderie, honour, excitement, adulation, an opportunity for glory, a chance to fight and kill the enemy. Death was a possibility, but in true Black Watch tradition, if it came it would be a glorious death. Fired by the evocative words of their charismatic commanding officer, Colonel Harry Walker, the 4th Battalion was prepared to take on the world. For the unemployed, the no-hopers and the down-and-outs, the war represented a chance, an opportunity to get out of a rut, to live a little, even if only for a short time. For the young, educated, editorial staff of the newspaper publishers, there was the appeal of adventure and a certain idealism. For the young men stuck in dead-end jobs in the factories and mills, it was a chance to get away, see the world, and soak up some of the reflected glory of the Black Watch legends.

Quite why Joe Lee joined up is not clear and needs close scrutiny. Almost 40 years old, with bronchial asthma, he was news editor of a local magazine, a respected journalist, an acclaimed local poet and artist and uncle to a much-loved niece. He had travelled extensively and enjoyed many experiences and was mature and worldly wise. No youthful haste influenced his decision. His mother, Christina, had died in 1913, but he still had his first niece, Chrissie, to cherish, as well as the love of his family. As far as is known, there was no great romance in his life at this time. Did he feel that his life was stagnant, his career at a dead end, his journeys travelled, his poetry written? Did he enlist on a point of principle, or through idealism, or did he see it as a last great adventure? Professionally he would certainly have missed the banter and office camaraderie in the weeks following the mass exodus of his colleagues from Leng's, as they rushed to volunteer with the Black Watch. Or did he feel duty-bound to use all his skills to help in the war effort – from his physical presence to his skill with pen and pencil? Perhaps the truth is a combination of all these factors. Whatever his reasons, the war inspired him to produce an incredible quantity of high quality war poetry and sketches, often under appalling conditions.

Those that enlisted seeking adventure, excitement and fear would not be disappointed. The Territorials of the 4th Battalion, The Black Watch were honoured to link up with the regulars of the 1st and 2nd Battalions, to form part of the Bareilly Brigade, Meerut Division, which comprised mainly Indian troops. Gurkhas, Dogras, the 58th Rifles and the Black Watch formed an exotic, but highly potent force of excellent ground troops, and within weeks of landing in France they were engaged in action. The Battle of Neuve Chapelle was a taste of the reality of war for the raw inexperienced 4th Battalion. General Sir Douglas Haig authorised a massive artillery strike against the German lines, followed by an advance involving 48 battalions. Fortunately for the 4th Battalion their involvement was largely in a support function, carrying provisions and ammunition. Nevertheless, for the first time they came under live fire and experienced life in the trenches, with shell bursts covering everything in mud and gore; the stench and smoke; the sting of cordite and the numbing cold. This was the harsh truth of conflict. Groups of bodies were found without a mark, felled by the sheer force of the explosion of a large shell, while others were torn apart, with limbs hanging from the trees and barbed wire. A group of Germans surrendered, then opened fire, although their treachery was punished with instant death as the British retaliated. Cowardice and desertion met with swift retribution.

A damaged crucifix at Neuve Chappelle, photographed after the war. The picture has elements in common with the image that inspired Lee's poem 'La Croix Rouge: A Wayside Calvary in Flanders'.

After one action Lee's company were commanded to assemble at a nearby French farm and were drawn up to form a square. The commanding officer announced that one of their own was being accused of cowardice in the face of the enemy. The man was marched into the square dressed in the uniform of an artilleryman, having being stripped of his Black Watch uniform in disgrace. As the charges were read out, Lee recalled that the silence was deafening. Not a man moved as they stared implacably into space, the silence broken only by the scratching of hens on the farmyard floor. The officer's voice, clear and strong, announced a guilty verdict, and sentenced the man to death. The sentence was later commuted, but every man was well aware that the ceremony was a clear indication that cowardice or desertion would not be tolerated in the ranks. Sadly the offender did not heed the lesson and later repeated the offence and was sentenced to death and shot.

The Fighter Writers initially tried to keep together while in France and three of them became inseparable. They were Linton Andrews, the 29-year-old news editor of the *Dundee Advertiser*, Joe Lee, the 39-year-old editor of *The People's Journal* , and 21-year-old John (Jack) Beveridge Nicholson, a talented staff writer at *The People's Journal*. Andrews and Nicholson started writing joint reports of their experiences and sending them to the *Dundee Advertiser*. The *Daily Mail* also received them and Lord Northcliffe, the owner, much impressed, believing the reports to be the work of one man, vowed to give the writer a job at the end of the war. Andrews and Nicholson had unofficial permission to complete their reports and were, from time to time, given access to classified information. In the meantime Joe Lee was writing moving poems about the war, describing every detail of life at the front, from the terrible conditions and experiences, to the humour and spirit of the men. He sent the poems back home, where they were published in the *Dundee Advertiser* and avidly read by the townspeople. Lee did not keep a journal during this time but relied on his poetry, supported by pencilled sketches, to convey his feelings.

Lee's poems provoked a great response among the people of Dundee, many of whom were inspired to write poetry of their own about the war. This notable phase in Dundee's cultural history has been recorded for posterity in a published volume of 1915 works called *Sword and Pen*, compiled by Dr Hilda Spear and Bruce Pandrich of Dundee University. This was intended to commemorate the Scottish soldiers who died at Loos in 1915, but is representative of the immense talent of writers in the Dundee area during the early part of the war.

During one action, after a particularly nasty exchange, two wounded men were left crying out in agony in No Man's Land. Sniper and machine gun fire raked the area, and the stretcher-bearers were reluctant to venture forth again; they had already lost one man killed and another wounded. Captain Boase, the same officer who had questioned Andrews's loyalty at the Drill Hall in

Dundee, was desperate for some rescue mission to be mounted. He asked Andrews to go, and he said yes without hesitation, then Lee and Nicholson agreed to go with him. Under persistent fire, they ventured across the open field, passing the half body of a German officer whose other half was in the British trenches, and the headless body of one of the Indian troops. Bodies were strewn everywhere, as if they had dropped from the skies and lay crumpled where they fell. Eventually they reached one of the injured men and returned safely with him. As they went back for the next casualty the sniper fire increased, in retribution for the success of the first rescue. When the three friends reached the second man they discovered that he was German. For men of courage and principle that made no difference and they helped the injured soldier to safety, despite the dangerous conditions. Joe Lee, modest as ever, does not mention his involvement in this incident in any of his writings.

Lee's colleagues at the front remember that he did not seem to need much sleep. Many times they would wake beside him, or near to him, to find him, sketchbook in hand, drawing scenes or composing poems. His quiet authority and composure endeared him to his colleagues. Andrews once said of him:

> [He was a] great character, the best loved man in the Battalion, apart from Colonel Walker, good hearted, would do anything for a comrade, keeps morale high and civilised standards, irrespective of the stench of death, helps retain a sense of perspective and can be relied upon to liven up get togethers with stories, songs or dramas.

Joe Lee was obviously a good man to have in a crisis.

Outside the major battles, even minor troop movements would provoke an exchange of fire that endangered the lives of the soldiers. On one occasion, part of the battalion had to proceed in single file and then, one by one, jump a ditch while snipers took pot shots at them like a fairground stall shoot. Waiting in line to jump it was simply a matter of chance whether you survived or not – one man died, and two were wounded. When the battalion later took up guard duties at the cross roads at La Croix Rouge in Flanders, which featured a Christ-like statue hanging from a cross, Lee, inspired by the effigy, wrote a haunting poem that was accompanied by a sketch. The poem begins:

Joe Lee's sketch of the crucifix to accompany his poem.

LA ROUGE CROIX

EBIT DE TABAC
No 725

Joseph Lee
Flanders 1915

Two thousand years since Christ was crucified;
Since thorn and nail did torment that frail flesh:
Again I see
Him hangéd on a tree,
And crucified afresh!

Once more that darkness over all the land;
The graves – *the graves are full* – they
give up not their dead:
The bitter cup
Is lifted up,
The crown pierces His head.

The last two verses of this ten-verse poem run:

Proud Kaiser, who has drowned the world in tears,
And deluged all the earth with reddest rain –
Christ's brow is torn
With crown of thorn –
Thine bears the brand of Cain!

O King in name, who might have been in deed,
Who chose the darkness rather than the light:
I see thee go
Forth from thy foe –
And it is night!

Shortly afterwards, Andrews, Lee and Nicholson were walking together when a shell landed between them. It remained unexploded and the three friends took their good fortune to be a sign. During those first few weeks Lee joined Andrews as a Lance Corporal and was very quickly elevated to the rank of Sergeant.

Despite the camaraderie and the promotions, Lee wrote a wonderful moving poem, called 'The Half Hour's Furlough', in which the narrator dreams of Dundee and home. It begins:

> I thought that a man went home last night
> From the trench where the tired men lie,
> And walked through the streets of his own old town –
> And I thought that the man was I.

The poet walks around his old haunts in Dundee, including St Mary's Tower and the 'old Arcade', before visiting a girlfriend:

> Till I came to the place of my long, long love,
> Where she lay with her head on her arm;
> And she sighed a prayer that the dear Lord should
> Shield my body from all harm.
>
> Ae kiss I left on her snow-white brow
> And ane on her raven hair,
> And ane, the last, on her ruby lips,
> Syne forth again I fare.

He goes to the home that he hopes one day to return to, and then to his mother's grave:

> Then I came to the glade where my mother was laid,
> 'Neath the cypress and the yew:
> And she stood abune, and she said 'My son,
> I am glad that your heart was true.'

The last verse brings the cold light of day, as the poet awakes to the reality of his situation:

> Then I awoke to the sound of guns,
> And in my ears was the cry:
> 'The Second Relief will stand to arms!'
> And I rose – for that man was I.

There were lighter moments to lessen the gravity of the soldiers' situation. Lee and his two comrades made friends with a local girl called Rosalie and her mother, and they would visit them for coffee from time to time. Later, shortly before the Battle of Aubers Ridge and the Festubert Salient in May 1915, the women kindly invited the three writers for a dinner of spaghetti, cold dumplings and figs, which was welcome relief from the usual army fare.

Despite this civilised and welcome interlude, Lee's maturity and experience are very evident in the poignant poem 'The Green Grass', written in the trenches just before the action at Aubers Ridge. Not for him a blinkered charge to glory, but a cool, measured assessment. He knew exactly what he was feeling and realised that the coming battle might be his last, as indeed it proved for many of his colleagues. Lee's poem left little doubt that he was very aware of what they were about to do:

THE GREEN GRASS

The dead spake together last night,
   And one to the other said:
   'Why are we dead?'

They turned them face to face about
   In the place where they were laid:
   'Why are we dead?'

'This is the sweet, sweet month o' May,
   And the grass is green o'erhead –
   Why are we dead?

'The grass grows green on the long, long tracks
   That I shall never tread –
   Why are we dead?

'The lamp shines like the glow-worm spark,
   From the bield where I was bred –
   Why am I dead?'

The other spake: 'I've wife and weans,
        Yet I lie in this waesome bed –
        Why am I dead?

'O, I hae wife and weans at hame,
        And they clamour loud for bread –
        Why am I dead?'

Quoth the first: 'I have a sweet, sweet heart,
        And this night we should hae wed –
        Why am I dead?

'And I can see another man
        Will mate her in my stead,
        Now I am dead.'

They turned them back to back about
        In the grave where they were laid: –
        'Why are we dead?'

'I mind o' a field, a foughten field,
        Where the bluid ran routh and red –
        Now I am dead.'

'I mind o' a field, a stricken field,
        And a waeful wound that bled –
        Now I am dead.'

They turned them on their backs again,
        As when their souls had sped,
        And nothing further said.

                    * * * * *

The dead spake together last night,
        And each to the other said,
        'Why are we dead?'

The Battle of Aubers Ridge was vicious and bloody, with heavy casualties on both sides. The Black Watch attack went in over open ground following a comparatively unsuccessful artillery bombardment. German machine-gun fire was devastating, and the Bareilly Brigade of Black Watch and Indian troops was cut to pieces. The Seaforths and the Gurkhas suffered badly – one charge, halted yards from the parapet by heavy machine-gun fire, left bodies strewn around like sandbags. The heavy German Maxim belt-fed machine gun could fire 600 rounds per minute, literally scything through anything in its path. It was estimated to have the equivalent firepower of 80 rifles. By the time the 4th Battalion moved up to the front line the area resembled a killing field. Andrews, Lee and Nicholson, realising that this was probably the end, shook hands and said their goodbyes. At the very last moment, a senior officer arrived and was amazed to find that the Territorials were about to attack a position that the regulars had been unable to take. He cancelled the order to attack. The three friends were spared once again.

It was in a trench in Flanders on 18 June 1915 that Lee, having experienced first hand the horror, futility and brutality of war, could finally relate to his grandfather, Sergeant David Lee. He wrote the poem '1815–1915: One Hundred Years Ago To-day' to express his feelings of kinship with his dead ancestor (see Prologue).

After the losses at Aubers Ridge and Festubert the battalion had a few weeks rest to lick its wounds, regroup and recuperate. Lee continued to send his poems to Dundee and Andrews and Nicholson were pursuing their role as unofficial war correspondents. The warm weather was a blessing and enabled the men, at times, to sleep out in the open; sometimes in barns, in haystacks or in the woods; anywhere to get away from the rats, the lice and the mosquitoes. Summer orchards, fields, wild flowers and farms were welcome breaks from the hardship of life in the trenches. The three men enjoyed their friendship, forged in adversity. Sustained by their total support for each other, it seemed that no matter what struggles lay ahead, together they would overcome them.

However, on 15 July 1915 something happened which put an end to the singing, the jesting and the optimism. During a rest and recuperation period, several of the men were fortifying the trench parapet, filling sand bags and generally bolstering the defences. At one point in the exercise John Nicholson, or 'Nik', as he was sometimes known, climbed onto the top of the parapet to rearrange the bags. A sharp-eyed sniper took aim and shot him close to the heart. He fell back into the trench, blood oozing from the wound. A corporal who went to help him after the first shot was killed by a second bullet. Lee and Andrews held Nicholson and tried desperately to help him, but he died in their arms. Shocked by the sudden and dramatic loss of their friend they carried him from the trench and recovered his personal belongings to send home to his family. They found several letters – some unfinished, some smeared with blood – and a luggage label with a funny message written on it from his girlfriend, which he always wore close to his heart. They tried to clean some of the letters and the undamaged ones they sent to his family. John Nicholson, or Nik, or Jack, as Lee called him, was, despite his frail physique, mentally strong and would be sorely missed. He was buried at St Vaast Post in an orchard under two apple trees, alongside Corporal Hutchinson, who had tried to save him. Lee and Andrews were grief-stricken, knowing that things would never be the same again. Lee wrote 'Marching' as a tribute to his dear friend, who had been almost like a son to him.

MARCHING

Marching, marching,
On the old-time track;
Soldier song upon my lip,
Haversack upon my hip,
Pack upon my back;
Linton on my left hand,
On my right side Jack –
Marching, marching,
Steel swung at my thigh,
Marching, marching,
Who so gay as I?

(Left, left!)

Marching, marching,

On the same old track;

Sorrow gnawing at my heart,

Mem'ry piercing like a dart,

Care perched on my back;

Linton on my left hand –

But, alas! poor Jack!

Marching, marching,

Quietly does he lie,

Marching, marching,

Who so sad as I?

(Left, left – *LEFT!*)

The battalion had been bloodied, and had experienced the death of friends and dreadful condition. The idea of the glory of war was a far-off memory. Joe Lee's poetry, appearing regularly back home, together with the publication of huge casualty lists, started to bring home to the public just how costly the war was proving in terms of human life.

To break the monotony during lulls in the fighting Joe Lee would sometimes give recitals, often featuring a favourite poem and the mouth organ, with live sound effects supplied by another soldier. This usually raised morale and gave the men a few laughs.

Lee often wrote cramped up in the trenches in appalling conditions. This hands-on experience permeates all his work, and allows the reader to see through the poet's eyes. It is, in its own way, brilliant war reporting by an experienced journalist. Lee captures every detail of the experience of life in the trenches, and by no means all of his poems can be classified as being about 'the horror of war'. His work is much more wide-ranging, and his poetic voice has many moods. For example, Lee wrote a poem about a comrade, called 'Macfarlane's Dug-out'. It tells, in a light and humorous tone, of a dug-out that Macfarlane fashioned for himself:

He shored it up with timber, and he roofed it in with tin,

Torn from the battered boxes that they bring the biscuits in –

(He even used the biscuits, but he begs I should not state

The number that he took for tiles, the number that he ate!) –
He shaped it, and secured it to withstand the tempest's shocks –
(I know he stopped one crevice with the latest gift of socks!) –
He trimmed it with his trenching-tool, and slapped it with his spade –
A marvel was the dug-out that Macfarlane made.

The poem accurately portrays the ingenuity that some men displayed when trying to create a little home comfort, although Lee admits, in a footnote to the poem, that he has exaggerated his account a little:

Postscript. – In the trenches, as will be readily understood, one has no continual abiding place. Consequently the dug-out of the picture is not the dug-out of the poem, and when I last looked in upon Macfarlane, he was swinging contentedly in a hammock of his own construction. It unfortunately falls to me to add a postscript of sadder import. Since the Advance of 25th September, my comrade has been counted among the missing.

Lee wrote the poem while under heavy bombardment, the ground shaking as he wrote; one can imagine the hammock swaying back and

Macfarlane in his dug-out.

forth. The reality of writing in the trenches is underscored by his later comment, that Macfarlane was sadly reported missing. He was later confirmed dead.

Lee and Andrews remained close and from time to time met up with old colleagues from Dundee, particularly the other Fighter Writers. Their first six months in France had been eventful, bringing experiences beyond their imagination, heartache and disillusion. The wholesale slaughter, the sheer horror of the trenches, and the heartache of personal loss, of Nicholson in particular, was coupled with the realisation that the war would not, as everyone had thought, be over quickly, and that soldiers were dispensable. Yet worse was still to come.

In the high summer Lee and Andrews often slept outside, preferring not to share a barn with lice-ridden men smoking and arguing. It must have brought back memories of their early recruitment days in the crowded, cramped, airless Drill Hall in Dundee. Lee would draw inspiration from the stars, a warm breeze, and the smell of hay or fruit and would enjoy reading his poetry out loud, often to Andrews. August in the trenches, however, was not a good time. Warmth and heavy rain provided the perfect conditions for mosquitoes, which made life in the trenches almost unbearable at times. Constant irritation and movement, together with the regular changes of sentries, resulted in a night's sleep amounting to three or four hours at best.

Linton Andrews had taken leave to return to Scotland and marriage. He returned just in time to take part in an engagement that would be forever inscribed in the history of the Black Watch. A comparatively unknown, insignificant village called Loos became a slaughterhouse for thousands of men. History records that there were 90,000 casualties. The British casualties, estimated at 60,000, were largely blamed on incompetence and poor leadership, which resulted in General Sir Douglas Haig replacing Field Marshall Sir John French as the British Commander-in-Chief.

A particular feature of the battle was the use of gas for the first time by British forces in support of an attack. The attempt backfired when the gas drifted back into the attacking force. In addition, the opening heavy bombardment had created huge clouds of smoke that hung around like a thick mist. Despite these difficulties the attack was pressed home and gains were made, but at a price. The Punjabis, the Gurkhas and the Black Watch suffered horrendous casualties. The Indian troops were much respected, not only for their bravery but also for their cheerful disposition. Despite the horrors they went about their duties – fighting, scouting or acting as stretcher-bearers – with dedication. Joe Lee was especially fond of his valued comrades and wrote 'Tik, Johnnie!' as a tribute to them. The poem gives an indication of the shared feeling between troops from a different continent and culture, yet suffering and enduring the same hardships as their British comrades.

ALLAH DAD

Allah Dad, an Indian soldier whose work on the front line was commemorated by Lee in his poem 'Tik, Johnnie!'

TIK, JOHNNIE!

'Tik, Johnnie!' (pronounce Teek) – the friendly and familiar salutation between the British Tommy and his Indian comrade-in-arms, heard so frequently during the first year of the war. Freely translated it means 'good', 'all right'; and many a time it seemed to render more tolerable, desperate and well-nigh intolerable conditions.

Allah Dad and Hira Singh,
You and I fought for the King!
Hajal Moka, Suba Khan,
You stood with us, man to man –
        Tik, Johnnie!

When we were tottering to our knees
Beneath a barbed cheval-de-frise,
And struggling through the muddy miles,
You'd meet us with a face all smiles
        And – Tik, Johnnie!

When we were crouching in the trench,
And choking in the smoke and stench,
The bullets falling like a flail,
You'd pass us with a friendly hail –
        Tik, Johnnie!

And when, on stretchers dripping red,
You bore the dying and the dead,
With pity in your wistful eye,
Your greeting seemed half sob, half sigh –
        Tik, Johnnie!

I've seen you leaning on a wall,
Your head smashed by a rifle ball;
You've smiled, and raised a hand, and cried
        Tik, Johnnie!
Then turned upon your side and died.

May Allah, when you go above,
Grant you the Heaven you would love;
And if our straying footsteps meet
Then free and friendly-like we'll greet –
        Tik, Johnnie!

As far as I am aware this tribute is the only war poem dedicated to the unselfish contribution and sacrifice of our Indian allies, many of whom paid the ultimate price at Loos.

Six battalions of the Black Watch fought at Loos but it was the 4th Battalion that suffered most, and their much-respected, highly popular leader Colonel Harry Walker, whose stirring words had helped speed his 4th Battalion from Dundee, was killed.

The bravery of the Scots on the Western Front was as great as anything from their proud history. At the command 'stand to', followed by a shrill whistle, or the cry of a bagpipe, the battalion went on the attack with cheer leaders calling out 'on the ba' Dundee', or shouting 'Marmalade!', a reference to Dundee's jam industry. Sadly, despite some successes they were cut down in their hundreds. The Black Watch officers, so proud of their uniforms, were brought down by their traditions: the gleaming red hackle on their bonnets, proudly won and worn, helped the German snipers identify the officers. They went about their task with deadly accuracy. Some reports claim 19 officers out of 20 were killed or wounded, others 20 out of 21; whichever is correct the statistics tell the story. After the battle all the men were allowed to wear the red hackle – a hard lesson learned.

The 4th Battalion had set out for France with a strength of 900 men. Despite replacements the force, prior to the Battle of Loos, had been reduced, excluding officers, to about 420 men. Of that number, 230 were killed or wounded at Loos. Only a few days before the battle, the 2nd and 4th Battalions of the Black Watch had been joined by the 5th Battalion for a sunny day of games and competitions in a field near the village of Estaines. Scots from Dundee and their near neighbours from Angus, friends, compatriots and comrades, joined together, if only briefly, in friendship. Just days later many of them were dead.

The 4th Battalion was decimated at Loos and when news of the casualties reached home, the impact was immense. The battalion, made up of local men – fathers, sons, brothers, uncles, nephews, workmates and neighbours – was truly Dundee's Own, and there was barely a household that did not receive a call, a telegram, a notification of death or wounding or, perhaps worse, a 'believed missing'. Everyone knew someone who had been killed. The 4th Battalion had been shattered and the remnants of it were temporarily amalgamated with the 5th Battalion.

In some quarters, of course, the battle was depicted as a victory. Local newspapers, understandably not wishing to recognise that such a terrible price had been paid for so little, gloried in the brave exploits of the Black Watch, not wishing to dwell on the tragedy. Despite the 'spin', however, there was no doubt that Dundee was a city in mourning.

Lee and Andrews survived the Battle of Loos, but the little group of Fighter Writers had suffered cruelly, and with promotions and movements of personnel it was getting more and more difficult to maintain contact. Nevertheless, despite their losses, the two remaining companies of the 4th Battalion fought on at Givenchy with the 2nd Battalion. Joe Lee was transferred, temporarily, to the Bareilly Brigade, but soon returned. The 4th Battalion, later replenished with fresh recruits, returned to strength.

The first few months of 1916 saw regular attack and counter-attack without any major battle. Nevertheless, for Lee and his comrades it was a terrible few months. Winter in the trenches, with sub-zero temperatures and heavy snow at times, followed by thaw and flooding, was punctuated by assault and counter-assault and hand-to-hand fighting in the enemy's trenches.

By now Joe Lee was relatively famous as the Black Watch poet. Revered by his comrades and acclaimed at home, his reputation as an excellent, honest poet was gaining momentum. So much so, that the publishing house of John Murray of London implored him to make a collection of his works for possible publication. Modest as ever, he took some persuading and was surprised when, impressed by his submissions, they offered and agreed a publishing deal. In April 1916 they published his first book of war poetry with illustrations, entitled *Ballads of Battle*. The book was relatively successful at the first run, becoming increasingly popular as the public started to take note, and eventually three further prints were run.

After the disaster at Loos, and given the heavy casualties sustained by the British forces during the early part of the war, it is surprising that many pundits believe that it was largely through the anti-war poetry of

Wilfred Owen, Siegfried Sassoon and others in late 1916 and early 1917 that the British public was alerted to the reality of the situation. Consider that *Ballads of Battle*, which was published in April 1916, contained poems written by Lee from the start of his war in February 1915. Consider also that many of them powerfully contradicted the romantic, patriotic notion of war – examples are 'The Dead Man', 'The Penitent', 'The Bullet', 'The Green Grass', 'Soldier Soldier' and 'The Combat'. The poems were undoubtedly popular and widely read, yet Lee was never thought of as being anti-war like such poets as Sassoon and Owen. Perhaps one reason for this is that Lee, with his journalist's background, sought to accurately represent the whole range of experiences of war, from the daily banter to the hideous casualties, without making more targeted political criticisms of those in power and the overall aims of the war. Lee's poetry and vision pre-dated that of his more illustrious, more celebrated peers. His poems of the early part of the war are an important part of the literature of the First World War that have not yet been fully appreciated. He accurately observed, portrayed and understood the fears, anxieties and needs of his comrades. *Ballads of Battle* is very rightly and fittingly dedicated 'To my comrades in arms'.

Lee continued to produce poetry and sketches of the war. Although he had become something of a celebrity after the publication of his book, his modesty would not allow him to curry favour. Some of the Fighter Writers had returned home to train for commissions but Joe refused several offers. Having survived for more than a year, his longevity and durability were much admired by his comrades.

The great offensive of 1916 was the Somme, where casualties amounted to 1.2 million. The reward was a piece of land measuring 20 miles by 7 miles. The carnage shocked the world and exacerbated anti-war feeling. For many it was difficult to be patriotic when young men were treated like cannon-fodder, being sacrificed for a strip of land that was waterlogged, pock-marked with bomb craters, devoid of all life and soaked in blood.

Lee spent November 1916 resting up near Ypres, but soon his battalion was on the move again. As they moved through Ypres, on Christmas Eve,

A BLACK WATCH DINNER IN BELGIUM

MENU

SARDINES ON TOAST

SOUP

SALMON

BEEF
POTATOES
BEANS

— HAGGIS —
WHISKY
PLUM PUDDING

RICE & FRUIT

COFFEE · CAKE
CIGARETTES, BISCUITS.

BON-BONS.

POPERINGHE
4TH JANUARY 1915

he sketched the shattered ruins of Ypres Cathedral. The New Year brought little respite but another wonderful sketch of a Black Watch dinner menu, dated 4 January 1917, shows a perplexed cook gazing at the proposed courses, which include sardines on toast, soup, salmon, potatoes, beans, beef, haggis, whiskey, plum pudding, rice, fruit, coffee, cake, biscuits, cigarettes and bon-bons. The sketch of the menu is signed by 17 men, including Linton Andrews and Pipe Major Dan McCleod, and gives a tantalising glimpse of luxury. There is no confirmation that all the items listed on the menu actually appeared on the table and it may have been wishful thinking on Lee's part. The rest of January 1917 was awful, with heavy rain, then frost, then more rain, resulting in the men being issued with gumboots. These kept out the rain, but because of their composition many of the troops developed trench foot, a painful condition that resulted in large expanses of skin coming away from the foot, leaving it raw and exposed.

Eventually, after rejecting several overtures, Joe finally agreed to return home to Scotland and train for a commission. He left for home on 26 February 1917, leaving Linton Andrews as the sole survivor of the original 4th Battalion. Lee had certainly grown weary of the continued struggle,

The menu for the Black Watch dinner, signed by the diners, 4 January 1917.

Lee's haunting sketch of the ruins of Ypres, Christmas Eve, 1916.

A photograph of
Ypres taken soon
after the end of the
war.

the degradation, the filth and death, and had perhaps marvelled at how he had survived. Often his poetry would reflect a longing for home or happier times. In 'The Sea: A Night Watch Above' he clearly remembers the his 'restless years' and his various sea voyages. It is a marvellous piece of imaginative writing, and it is incredible that such fine, sensitive poems could be written in the filth and stench of the trenches. Not for Lee the comfort of an armchair and a period of recuperation to sit and concentrate on composition and form. The poem is featured in his second book of war poetry, *Work-a-day Warriors,* which was published in 1917.

THE SEA: A NIGHT WATCH ABOVE

My soul is sick for the sea,
For the scudding ships,
For the rollers racing free,
For the winds that sting like whips,
For the winds that sting like whips,
For the winds that smack like wine:
O for a good ship on the sea,
If that good ship were mine.

Here is the night watch set,
And here do I take my stand,
Doing my spell at the parapet,
With my eye fixed on No Man's Land;
With my eye set on No Man's Land,
With my eye on that waste o' Hell,
But my heart alert for the full sail's fret
And the boom of the old ship bell.

I set my soul on an outward bound,
And I set the course by a star;
But I miss the swell beneath my feet,
As she noses for over the bar,
As she rises and dips at the bar,
As she pauses to sniff the gale;
To night I would circle the whole world round
With never a shorten sail!

I stand on the firing-step,
As I've stood on the fo'c'sle-head,
And I think of the sailors drowned I've known,
And the soldiers I've known who are dead,
Of my mates over there who are dead,
Of my mates who are graved in the sea,
And I think that if God gave me choice of graves,
I know what my choice would be!

The spindrift smites my face,
As there comes the lashing of rain,
And the gale whistles through the top-gallants
Like the cry of a soul in pain,
Like the cry of a soldier slain? –
Or a mariner in the sea? –
Ah! if God would but give me choice of death
I know what my choice would be!

'The Derelict' –
Lee's illustration to
accompany his
poem 'The Sea'.

However, there may have been another reason for Lee returning home to seek a commission. Perhaps he had one eye on the future, a future that perhaps at his age he had not dared contemplate. Ever since that day in 1911 when 12-year-old Dorothy Barrie won the music competition Joe, believing that she was talented, had taken an interest in her development. She moved to London to study music at the Royal Academy and he kept in touch with her.

Home from leave on one occasion, in an attempt to impress Dorothy, Joe took her to lunch. Whatever happened, perhaps nerves or a complication of his bronchial asthmatic condition, he suddenly, in the middle of lunch, was taken by a noisy, prolonged fit of coughing. She was not impressed. Fortunately there would be other occasions.

Leave times were precious but also unsettling, something that Lee vividly portrays in his poem 'Back to London: A Poem of Leave'. He writes of coming home on leave by train, of the hills, of sheep in fields, children waving from a gate, factory girls and station names. The first and last two verses summarise his anguish:

I have not wept when I have seen
My stricken comrades die;

I have not wept when we have made
  The place where they should lie;
My heart seemed drowned in tears, but still
  No tear came to my eye.

Eleven further verses describe the views from the train, intermingled with the pain of past experiences, and the poem ends:

I have not wept when I have seen
  A hundred comrades die;
I have not wept when that we shaped
  The house where they must lie –
But now I hide my head in my hand
  Lest my comrades see me cry.

These are the scenes, these the dear souls
  'Mid which our lot was cast,
To this loved land, if Fate be kind,
  We shall return at last,
For this our stern steel line we hold –
  Lord, may we hold it fast!

It seems incongruous to compare Joe Lee, smart, clean, freshly shaven and coiffured, having lunch in a London restaurant with an attractive young lady, with the man a week before or after fighting for his life in a hole in the ground. The trenches with their rats, lice, excrement and body parts exuding the stench of death and decay, and the desperation and frenzy of hand-to-hand fighting, were terrible, and that horror was thrown into sharp relief by the normality of leave. How could you walk out of the restaurant and step back into that hell? No wonder that some could not do so, and deserted.

Joe Lee had survived two years on the Western Front, which in itself was a remarkable achievement. Following his spell of training back home, he was gazetted second lieutenant in the King's Royal Rifle Corps and returned once again to the trenches. Although Lee had left his beloved

Black Watch and his close comrades, the 6th and 7th Battalions of the Black Watch, together with Lee's King's Royal Rifle Corps, as part of the British Third Army, would soon be fighting in the same massive engagement. A few months of light skirmishing helped Lee to adjust to his new responsibilities and the added burden of leadership. His reputation as a poet and artist, meanwhile, was reaching a wider audience. America had taken notice and was asking 'Who is this young poet fighting somewhere in France, no one seems to know.' Some of his poems had been published in national newspapers and magazines in Britain, and *Ballads of Battle* had won critical acclaim.

The sketch that appears beneath the dedication at the beginning of *Work-a-day Warriors*.

In Dundee a virtual industry of war poetry had evolved. Lee's poetry and the gallantry of Dundee's Own had stirred the senses of the populace, who responded in verse. The whole gamut of experience from lament to patriotism, from criticism to praise was covered. A number of poems were in fact about Joe Lee, whose experiences and thoughts were avidly followed by the townspeople. Highly regarded in the community, his communications were like beacons of light to the people. He was theirs and he was out there surviving; a symbol of hope still standing. During this time Lee's second book of war poems *Work-a-day Warriors* was about to be published, again dedicated 'To Him', meaning Lee's comrades, the soldiers. Is a second book ever as good as the first? Sequels are often a disappointment. But not Lee's *Work-a-day*

Warriors. Several powerful and incisive poems evoke experience, insecurity, disillusion and fragility. The much-acclaimed 'German Prisoners' swings from hate to an understanding of the futility of war, while 'Glad That I Killed Yer' chillingly portrays the realism of hand-to-hand fighting. Once again there are superb pencilled illustrations, of Marcelle, a waitress; a nurse; an Indian soldier; an Australian soldier; a tank; and Ypres on Christmas Eve – numerous observations, illustrated with the clarity of a camera, but retaining warmth and movement.

Joe Lee's drawing of a tank in action, made at the Somme in 1916.

At this point in his life Lee had attained a level of recognition and was being published in some anthologies, including *The Muse in Arms*, edited with an introduction by E.B. Osborn, along with such luminaries as Rupert Brooke, Robert Graves and Siegfried Sassoon, all of whom would be famed for their war poetry throughout their lives and, indeed, long afterwards.

In October 1917 Lee was moved to Heudicourt in command of 'A' Company, 10th Battalion, King's Royal Rifle Corps. Sporadic fighting in late October and early November was followed by tell-tale signs that something unusual was in the offing. British patrols reported that many familiar features, previously thought to have been hedges, large guns, ammunition dumps, latrines and other types of structure, were actually cleverly designed and camouflaged sites. The secret quickly became public: the British Third Army had moved almost 400 tanks into line to provide the thrust into part of the Hindenburg Line. A major battle, which would result in casualties approaching 100,000, was imminent and would erupt on 20 November 1917.

On 17 November Joe Lee wrote a letter, a beautifully illustrated letter, to his first niece Chrissie (Christina). It was the first time that he had written to her and one wonders whether he was prompted to write by a premonition of what was to come. Chrissie was eight years old, but her mother Kate had also given birth to a second daughter, Kathleen, in 1916. Joe now had two nieces. He finishes the letter 'with love to you and ma, Kathleen, Grace (Herman's wife), Auntie Nelly and Uncle Herman.'

Entitled 'A Little Letter to a Little Girl from the Firing Line, British Exped Force, France 17th November 1917', the letter begins with Joe telling Chrissie that ever since he has been in the war, not a day has gone by without him thinking of her, and this letter is 'all to yourself' because one of the first letters Chrissie ever wrote was to Joe 'all for myself'. He describes the journey which his letter will take before it reaches her and explains, and illustrates, his living quarters and dug-out. The letter is written while he sits on his bed, which consists of a few wooden boards, a blanket and his great coat, with his knees doubled up to his chin. He explains that when the letter is finished it will be placed in a jute sack and remarks that the sack was probably made in Dundee! The letter writing is interrupted by the call 'Dinner ready, sir' and Joe explains that he moves into the dining room, another dug-out with a table, two benches which are very wobbly and two candles. The dinner consists of soup, meat pie and, for the first time in the trenches, spaghetti, and a sort of pudding. He comments that the spaghetti reminded him of Chrissie's story about spaghetti in her letter. After finishing the dinner, which he says wasn't bad, he recommences the letter. He delightfully recounts that as he was drawing a picture of his dug-out for her, a little mouse came out from behind a sand bag so he included it in his illustration. Mice are fine, he says, but he doesn't like rats, two of which frequent his dug-out. Although he doesn't like them he tells her that they can't help being rats, and he has got used to sleeping among them. In mock anger he says to her that one of the rats crept in on tiptoe, stole a piece of candle and ate it!

Joe complains that when he got up at 2am for his spell of duty, he had to put on his helmet and box respirator, and find a cigarette, all in the dark. He illustrates and explains that going to bed is easy, you don't take off your clothes or boots and when your feet and boots are covered in mud you just place them in a sandbag. An intelligent, educated man, Joe can't help but explain how writing has evolved over the years from writing

The front page of Lee's long letter to his niece.

on tablets of stone at the time of Moses and the Ten Commandments. He explains how the American Indians wrote on birch bark and pieces of wood and asks Chrissie to get her mother, Kate, to read to her Longfellow's 'Hiawatha', which details the method of picture writing. He concludes by thanking Chrissie for sending a violet and encloses some wild flowers that he picked from the side of the trenches that morning, and he promises to write again. The end of the letter is illustrated with a fine self-portrait.

The self-portrait that appears at the end of Lee's letter to Chrissie.

Joe would write again, but in very different circumstances. The whole letter is a delightful piece, with seven supporting illustrations: a miniature work of art. Shortly after Lee wrote came the Battle of Cambrai. A massive British tank attack punched a huge hole in the German lines, but failure to capitalise on the success of the initial thrust resulted in a successful German counter-attack. Fighting continued until the Germans launched a final successful action on 30 November. The 10th Battalion King's Royal Rifle Corps, together with the 11th Battalion King's Royal Rifle Corps on its left and the 12th Division on its right, had on 29 November taken up position in trenches near Lateau Wood. The Germans launched a determined, decisive attack on the 12th Division, breaking through their lines and coming through the woods to get behind the 10th and 11th King's Royal Rifle Corps. Casualties were severe as the fighting intensified. The King's Royal Rifle Corps was exposed for the first time to machine-gun fire from aircraft. Nevertheless, despite their desperate plight, the four companies of the King's Royal Rifle Corps, including Lee's A Company, fought bravely against the odds. The Germans, having surrounded the British position, launched a final attack, which overwhelmed the defenders. After the battle stragglers drifted back to British lines, where the survivors of the four Companies were listed as four officers and 16 other ranks. Sixteen officers were believed missing or dead. Joe Lee was one of them. The whole action resulted in 44,000 British casualties, with German losses estimated at over 50,000. The result was stalemate.

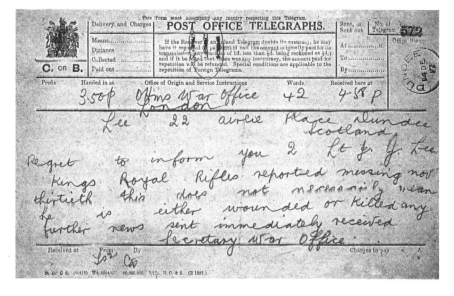

The telegram sent to Lee's brother Herman on 14 December 1917, which reported Lee missing.

On 14 December 1917 the Lee family received the dreaded news, which many Dundee families had received before them, in a telegram from the War Office. Accepted by his brother Herman, the telegram to Lee, at 22 Airlie Place, Dundee, said:

Regret to inform you 2nd Lt. J. Lee, King's Royal Rifles reported missing Nov. 30th. This does not necessarily mean he is either wounded or killed, any further news sent immediately received – Secretary, War Office.

The news hit the Lee family hard. They had just received the lovely letter addressed to Chrissie. Was their beloved brother dead, had Chrissie and Kathleen lost an uncle; had Dundee lost one of its favourite sons? Shortly afterwards Herman Lee received a letter from Lieutenant Colonel Sheepshanks, the commanding officer of the 10th Battalion King's Royal Rifle Corps, confirming the loss of Joe Lee. Sheepshanks explained that the Germans had cut off and surrounded the companies of his battalion, and that although they had little chance of survival they had fought splendidly. He said that all Joe's fellow officers were missing and he hoped that they were prisoners of war. Joe Lee, he said, had commanded A Company extremely well throughout the fighting and was a most valued officer, whose loss was felt tremendously. He concluded with deepest sympathy and with the sincere hope that 'your brother may be a Prisoner of War'.

Christmas 1917 was a fraught and tense time for the Lee family, not wanting to grieve but praying for Joe's delivery. When the joyous news, by way of telegram from Joe Lee via the Red Cross at Geneva, Switzerland, confirmed that he was indeed a prisoner of war, being held inside Germany, their prayers were answered. Joe asked in the telegram for a food parcel and underclothes and concludes, 'all well, waiting'. It was the best possible Christmas present for the Lee family back home in Dundee. Joe Lee's war was, however, over and he would spend Christmas 1917 as the guest of the German government.

CHAPTER FIVE

Prisoner of War

JOE LEE had taken the decision to surrender with a heavy heart. He, more than most, was aware of the proud history and reputation for bravery enjoyed by his countrymen. However, he was no 'General Custer' – there was no question of him risking the lives of his men in vain pursuit of personal glory. A Company, and the other companies, had fought to a standstill, losing many men in the process. They had been surrounded and further resistance was futile. At the end of the war Lee's Certificate of Discharge from the Secretary of the War Office confirmed that the decision to surrender was correct. Lee was exonerated from any blame.

Nevertheless, the actual moment, the point of surrender, must have been terrifying. Hours spent slaughtering one another and then one side offers itself to the other in an act of surrender, a plea for mercy fraught with danger. It was not unusual in such circumstances for the victors to shoot their prisoners in revenge for the loss of their own comrades, or simply because they could not cope with a group of prisoners. In that respect Joe Lee and his fellow officers and men were fortunate. Following capture they were moved to a German headquarters away from the front line and searched, particularly for weapons. Lee managed, during the march, to surreptitiously tear up and scatter military papers to avoid them falling into enemy hands. Later they were moved to the village of Caudrey, where the German guards prevented the local people from giving them food, despite the fact that the prisoners had not eaten for more than 30 hours.

They were billeted overnight in a factory and, after almost 48 hours, received their first meal of potatoes and beans. Later that day they theatrical culture among the prisoners. The French put on several plays, while the Irish, thanks to a Lieutenant Martin who had appeared at the Abbey Theatre in Dublin, put on Lady Gregory's *The Rising Of The Moon*. Incredibly, Martin had memorised the original play and wrote it down from memory. The Italians, inspired by Lee, put on *An Italian Vignette*, for which Lee painted a Venetian backcloth from memory. Other plays, such as G.B. Shaw's *How He Lied to Her* and *The Secret and the Brigand*, kept the happy band of thespians active and the four, sometimes five-strong orchestra coped excellently with their many challenges.

Lee was in his element. He designed the sets, painted the scenery, wrote, produced, created posters and generally would do anything to assist, and ensure, a successful production. By this time he had forged friendships with all and sundry.

From time to time prisoners would leave the camp and be replaced by others, sometimes disrupting the theatrical set-up or the duties assigned to more permanent residents. As fate would have it, Lee found himself reunited with a colleague, Lieutenant J.M. Hood from the Machine Gun Corps, who was also an employee on the *Dundee Advertiser*. The Dundee newspapers published a photograph of the two men taken in Carlsruhe. More exotic guests arrived in the form of sailors from Britain, America, Scandinavia, Australia and Japan. They had all been captured at various times following the sinking of their vessels by the German warship *Wolf*, and some had been prisoners on board the *Wolf* for more than a year. The genial Joe was interested in the Japanese and managed to get an invitation to their hut. While he was sketching some of their interesting, oriental faces, they told him the tragic story of their capture. Their ship, *The Hitachi Man*, had been sunk with severe loss of life and the survivors picked up and imprisoned aboard the German ship. The captain, in true Japanese tradition, believed that the only way that he could redeem himself was by committing suicide. One night he left his cabin on the *Wolf* and, while the ship was picking its way, in the darkness, through the ice floes off Iceland, he jumped overboard.

Another sailor, Captain Meadons, whose ship had also been sunk by the *Wolf*, told Lee of his attempts to take revenge. During his long stay on board the German ship he had frequently, following a bath, emptied the water into the open sea, together with a bottle containing information about the *Wolf*. The Germans eventually found him out and from then on he was always searched before he was allowed to take a bath.

Despite these interesting and often full days, there was an ever-present danger, even though it was not very evident in the first few weeks. The location of the prison camp, virtually in the centre of town, did render it vulnerable if an air strike was attempted on the town itself. One air raid in 1916 killed 100 civilians, mostly women and children. A number of trees just outside the camp bore the heavy scars of shrapnel hits. Raids continued and in one week, there were eight attacks so close to the camp that shrapnel and bomb fragments rained down into the site, hitting the roofs of the huts. There were usually warnings of attack, sirens and whistles that were sometimes greeted with loud cheers from the patriotic prisoners. One raid sadly resulted in bombing very near to the camp, which caused fatal casualties among factory girls in the town. The prisoners had a grandstand view of the action, but had to suffer the sight of a British plane being shot down, while another crashed. Two of the bodies of the airmen were recovered and a funeral service was arranged, which Lee attended. Despite the fact that enemy aircraft had caused suffering to their town, the funeral service for the two airmen was well attended and tears were shed by the women.

Very soon spring and early summer showed Carlsruhe in a better light. Blossoms, carried on the wind, would fall into the camp and Lee, with his appreciation of nature, was uplifted by the sight of majestic horse chestnut trees in full foliage among the buildings. Greenery sprang from crevices in the concrete, lending colour to the otherwise drab corners. The warmth of June was quietly spent, the nationalities teaching each other their languages and Lee enjoying a memorable Sunday dinner given by Italian friends; then came the news on 5 July that he was to be transferred to another prisoner of war camp, at Beeskow, near Berlin. Strangely, although he had spent 200 days as a prisoner at Carlsruhe, and had made many friends and played a key role in maintaining the morale of the inmates, his only feelings on being told of his transfer were of exhilaration. Or was it merely his old wanderlust, that restlessness, the desire to wander round the earth, that was raising its head once more?

Later, and fortunately peacefully, the Commandant and the Mayor were both deposed and further relaxations in the prison regime were permitted.

Cinematography shows were held in an old hall, during which a British officer and a German soldier took turns playing the piano to accompany the film. An acrobatic act of father, mother and three sons entertained all the prisoners and their guards and disclosed to Lee that they were a travelling act who had played in England and had been stuck in Sweden when the war broke out. It was all quite surreal. Lee was allowed to wander around the streets unaccompanied, and on one occasion encountered a motor wagon, covered in fir tree branches and packed with German soldiers, which had come straight from the front. Although they stared hard at him, perhaps in disbelief, there was no hostility. Joe Lee and a fellow officer, Captain Tim Sugrue, passed a building near the railway crossing while out on a walk and through the open door saw the salon, covered with flags, bunting and red roses. They could see on the small raised stage a little orchestra, piano, violin and cello, playing music, while about 80 couples, German solders and their womenfolk, danced tirelessly, seemingly oblivious to the stresses of the time and the growing chaos as the war moved towards a conclusion.

Lee relished having a companion, in Sugrue, who shared his wanderlust and curiosity, and they set off to visit another tiny village at Radinkerdorf. Finding a small café, they sat down as the proprietor, an old lady, made them coffee. When she asked them where they were from, they replied honestly that they were from 'the prison'. On learning that they were prisoners, she replied, 'We are all human'. She begged them to tell her why they were at war, but the men had no answer for her.

On another trip to another village, Friedland, Lee and Sugrue had an encounter with a German soldier fresh from the front. They were sat by the warm stove, having a coffee, when he entered the café and instantly there was a kinship. There was no hostility, just a recognition of the futility of war. He told them, as they sipped coffee, that his company had retreated quickly from the front in panic, and in the rush for safety they had left most of their equipment behind. As he got up to leave he shook hands with them and expressed his relief that the war was almost over.

It was now early December and Lee and Sugrue decided to take French leave and head for Berlin, some two and a half hours away by train. They thought the opportunity to see the city too good to miss. However, they were unaware of developments in Berlin. It was a dangerous, highly charged place, with revolution in the air and on the streets, certainly no place for two uniformed, unaccompanied British officers. They quickly got a taste of what was in store for them when they saw newspaper headlines being read by their fellow train passengers. One headline jumped out at them: '14 dead, 50 wounded in street fighting in Berlin'.

Captain Tim Sugrue, Lee's companion on excursions from the prison.

Back in March the Germans had launched a massive offensive, almost a do-or-die effort, which had almost succeeded. The Allies had, however, recovered from the shocks of the initial thrust and had slowly pushed the Germans back until Germany was staring defeat in the face. As the Allied advance continued, many Germans realised that the war was lost and that further resistance was futile. In October, German sailors in Kiel refused orders to fight and openly mutinied. The unrest spread to Hamburg and Bremen, and, in early November, to Munich. The Kaiser eventually agreed to abdicate on 8 November, when he was persuaded that he could no longer rely on the loyalty of the army. Fighting on the Western Front ceased with the signing of an armistice on 11 November.

Revolution was in the air and gradually spread to Berlin. Left-wing extremists of the Social Democratic Party had disagreed with their party's attitude to the war and believed that the way forward was through the people, the workers, rising up in rebellion. Two of the leaders, Karl Liebknecht and Rosa Luxemburg, had previously been found guilty of treason and jailed for their views. After being released they raised the profile of their communist-based Sparticusbundes Party with a series of meetings, designed to incite the people to take action. The Social Democratic Government, utilising mercenaries, was determined to crush them; and this set the scene for the events in Berlin that Lieutenant Joe Lee and Captain Tim Sugrue would witness.

As they left the train in Berlin, a couple, noticing their uniforms, sidled up to them and whispered 'Thank God Britain won', before slipping silently back into the throng. Lee and Sugrue had breakfast in the station – fried haddock, salad and coffee, three marks – then started to walk slowly into the city centre. People glanced at them from time to time and sometimes hesitated, wondering perhaps why two uniformed British officers were walking around unguarded. On occasions people asked them if they were part of an advanced army of occupation.

Luckily for Lee, Sugrue shared, to a certain extent, his cultural tastes, and they tried to seek out Berlin's treasures. They located the picture gallery, which was closed, but they entered the sculpture gallery and managed to persuade the manager to let them see some of the fabulous Greek sculptures. Lee particularly remembers a Grecian work of art dating from 480 BC which had been taken from the Louvre in 1870. He suggested to the manager that with the way events were turning out it might well find its way back to the Louvre!

As the two men walked around the town, it was clear that all was not well. Large posters in red and white, of soldiers beating drums, shouting wildly with their eyes blazing and sailors waving flags signalling distress were displayed in public places. Many of the buildings bore evidence of a struggle; machine-gun bullets had carved out furrows in the stone of buildings and the single dents of rifle fire were everywhere. Palaces, museums, memorials and bridges, it seemed, had all been affected by the revolt. People appeared dejected and all strategic points were manned by soldiers and sailors wearing distinctive white armbands. These men also patrolled the streets, and although curious about the two strolling British officers, they were generally friendly. Ironically, the Royal Opera House was advertising Verdi's *Othello* that night and the following night was putting on *Rigoletto*, clearly determined to go ahead no matter what. Perhaps a sign saying 'performances subject to revolution' should have been displayed.

Lee and Sugrue continued their tour of the city, visiting the Reichstag, which looked deserted, and then examining the Hindenberg statue, which looked somehow forlorn. Civilians and troops could be glimpsed milling about, as the officers moved from street to street, but there was no manifestation of terror or violence. Suddenly, they noticed a huge, silent, sombre procession slowing moving their way; red banners fluttering in the breeze, red banners trailing on the floor. It was the Sparticusbundes Party with the charismatic Liebknecht and the powerful orator Rosa Luxemburg at its head. Lee realised that this group, the Spartacists, had suffered 14 dead and over 50 wounded during the previous day's events. The procession ground to a halt close to where the two officers were standing, and as a large crowd gathered Liebknecht launched into his address. Arms waving frantically, eyes blazing, face livid with the effort, Lee remembered him as 'a volcanic figure with the distorted mouth of a Greek tragic mask'. He was inciting the crowd and was well into his stride when screams were heard and the crowd started to stampede in all directions. The government had sent in motor wagons full of troops of the Security Service of the Social Democratic Party, complete with machine guns.

Sugrue was anxious to leave the area, reasoning that if the shooting started, force of habit would result in the easily identifiable British officers being among the first targets. Fortunately the troops, after the previous day's slaughter, had been instructed only to shoot in self-defence. The demonstration was broken up peacefully and Lee caught a final glimpse of Liebknecht and Luxemburg being led away. Weeks later the news was released to the world that both Liebknecht and Luxemburg had been killed. Many believed that they had been murdered by the police after being arrested.

Lee and Sugrue escaped and sought shelter in a small café, where they encountered a Russian who lived in Berlin. He told them of the anarchy in the city and said that he would be delighted if they would visit his home before finally leaving Berlin. It was a question of finance whether they could stay the night in the city or return to Beeskow. As luck would have it they had no difficulty in finding a hotel within their price range, and indeed enjoyed considerable luxury. In a scene that could have come straight out of an Elstree Studios film, two British officers enjoyed a comfortable night in a plush, luxuriously pillowed bed in a hotel in Berlin, and then pulled on the bell rope to summon a waiter for morning coffee while studying the railway timetable for the return to the prison camp. They decided that they would have time to attend Sunday Mass at the St Hedenick cathedral and afterwards try to visit the home of the Russian whom they had met the previous day. While trying to find the street where he lived they were assisted by one of the sailors who was helping to guard the streets. He proudly informed them that he had been to Hartlepool and Gateshead and took great care to ensure that they were put on the correct tramcar.

Eventually they found the house and the Russian and his family were thrilled to see them and treated them with great hospitality. Nevertheless, they were advised to leave Berlin on the afternoon train as the revolution was gaining momentum, and it was feared that further and more severe fighting was imminent. It was the intention of the Russian family to escort the officers to the station and then return to their house and literally 'batten down the hatches'. A nephew volunteered to accompany them, and as they travelled by tram to the station their vehicle was passed by a motor car full of sailors and soldiers throwing out copies of a pamphlet, one of which Lee grabbed. It was a paper headed *Red Flag*, from the Sparticusbundes Party, announcing a mass meeting and listing a number of speakers, including Rosa Luxemburg, Karl Liebknecht, Levi and Duncker. They had not been deterred by the deaths of colleagues or threats from the Government security forces. In a very short time, however, with their leaders dead and the Government cracking down mercilessly, the revolution would crumble and fade away.

Lee and Sugrue eventually caught the evening train to Beeskow and, in a delightful moment, had to ring the bell at the camp gates to be allowed in. The guard glanced at them with a knowing eye, and allowed them in without comment.

The following day they were informed that they were free and started to pack their belongings, meagre as they were. In Lee's case the most precious of all his possessions were his journals, diary and sketches. As the prisoners marched through the gates of Beeskow the local people gathered to wave goodbye and to shake their hands. The five months spent in this small camp had been far from arduous, more frustrating than harrowing.

That night Lee once again found himself in Berlin, but this time very briefly, as the prisoners were placed in a convoy of hackney carriages and driven through the dark, deserted streets to the railway station and thence to Warnemunde and the sea. The *Prins Christian*, a Danish ship, was waiting, and the escorting German officer read out the names of each of the prisoners, who responded and then walked up the gangplank to freedom. It was appropriate that the German officer was Lieutenant Kruggel, who had always displayed the utmost courtesy. Once every man had been accounted for, Kruggel shook hands with all the officers, saluted them and slowly walked down the gangplank, his duty honourably done.

Lee's adventures, however, were not yet over. The journey home was circuitous to say the least. The ship was bound for the Baltic Sea, an area once visited by Lee, and Denmark. Following the sea voyage he would be transferred to Copenhagen, then to Leith and home. Lee enjoyed the sea voyage: the wind, the salt fresh air and the open spaces brought back memories of the travels of his restless years, even though it was December. The wind, although welcome, was icy cold and whipped through clothing. But Joe Lee was free at last. Once on Danish soil he and the men transferred to the train for Copenhagen.

During the train journey Lee noticed a little boy, pale, thin and obviously unwell, so he gave up his seat to enable him to rest. The two gentlemen, both Danish, who accompanied the boy, were very grateful to Lee and during the conversation told him who the boy was, and the purpose of their journey. The young boy, aged nine, was the youngest son of Herr Duncker, Professor of Philosophy at Berlin University, and one of the leaders of the Sparticusbundes Party. They were moving him to Copenhagen for his own safety and to treat his malnutrition. He already had an elder brother living safely in Copenhagen. Lee had witnessed the death

A contemporary review of *A Captive at Carlsruhe*, Joe Lee's account of his time as a prisoner of war

A CAPTIVE AT CARLSRUHE.

Lieutenant Joseph Lee, whose writings as soldier, poet, and artist are well known not only in Dundee but in a wide circle elsewhere, has produced another book of great interest. In this work Lieutenant Lee describes in that vivid, realistic style of which he is a pastmaster, the privations and hardships he suffered as a captive at Carlsruhe and other German prison camps. His illustrations of the grim, factory-like places in which he was confined, of his companions in misfortune, and of his jailers—some of them humane enough, while some were as pompous and aggressive as Germans can be—are quite as clever and entertaining as the narrative.

But the author had many compensations. His literary and artistic gifts were by no means wasted in captivity, leading him to play an important and useful part in the little plays by which the prisoners endeavoured to break the monotony of their existence. He wrote a drama for them and also took on himself the Pooh-Bah character of "scene-painter, scene-shifter, poster-artist, actor, and prompter." Further, he was appointed librarian of a small collection of books discovered in one of the camps, and as it included sundry portions of the Pickwick Papers, readings were started and enjoyed. Fate took the captives to Beekow and Berlin, where they were witnesses of the revolution following the armistice. With a genuine human touch the Lieutenant refers to his feelings on being released. There was not, he says, that immediate and amazing emotion of exultation he had imagined and anticipated. "In after years, however, there will be the full realisation that shall move to tears." On the whole, a most admirable book.—John Lane, London.

throes of the Spartacists in Berlin and feared for the life of the young boy's father.

When the long journey home was finally completed, Lee received a hero's welcome. Dundee's own poet, the people's inspiration during the dark days of the war, had survived and was back among them in his beloved city. He had been incarcerated for just over a year and on his return, he more than most, recognised the awful sacrifice, the cost that his home town had borne in the war. But there was no doubt that Christmas 1918, spent in the bosom of his family, no matter the absence of luxuries, was a far better prospect than Christmas 1917 in Carlsruhe, as a prisoner of war.

CHAPTER SIX

The Fate of the Fighter Writers

THE soldiers gradually returned home following demobilisation and, for many families, the return of a loved one ended months, or indeed years, of agony. More, many more in Dundee, had no such joy, just a permanent ache exacerbated by seeing the joy in others. As Lee wandered around the town he could see that there was little evidence of the war, no damage, no bullet-scarred walls, no bomb-shattered buildings, but scars there were nonetheless. Familiar faces were missing from shops, the market, buses, street corners and the factories; many young people, lads and girls, and women and older men had filled the positions vacated by Dundee's dead.

The major manpower contribution to the 4th Battalion Black Watch during the war had included the men from the jute mills and the jam factories and the third 'J', journalism. Dundee had two major publishers at the outbreak of the First World War, John Leng & Co. and D.C. Thomson, which between them had employed several thousand people.

John Leng, a Hull man, was responsible for the rejuvenation of the *Dundee Advertiser*, which had been founded in 1801. When he was selected from among 70 candidates for the post of editor in 1851, the *Advertiser* was in a state of stagnation, lacking direction and strategy. Within a few short years he had turned it into a highly respected local paper with a national identity. In 1859 the paper moved to new premises in Bank Street and John Leng was offered a partnership by the grateful owners and eventually the name John Leng & Co. became synonymous with publishing.

The previous year, 1858, the very successful *The People's Journal*, a weekly newspaper, became the largest selling newspaper in Scotland and in 1861 the *Dundee Advertiser* was produced as a daily newspaper. Another successful launch was *The People's Friend*, in 1869, which quickly rivalled London's quality periodicals. *The Evening Telegraph*, a halfpenny daily newspaper launched in 1877, was eventually merged with the *Evening Post* in 1900. By this time John Leng himself had moved very much into the political corner and was elected Liberal Member of Parliament for Dundee in 1889. Several of his own books clearly outlined his views: *Dealing With the Unemployed* in 1886, *Home Rule All Round* in 1890, and *Nationalisation – The Dream of The Labour Party* in 1895. He was a firm believer in Home Rule and a strong supporter of worker's rights, believing for example that working hours were excessive, and he advocated the appointment of female inspectors in factories and workshops. He was knighted in 1893 and was still Dundee's MP when he died on a visit to California in 1906. Although he was born in Hull his ashes were returned to Newport, to the area that he had served so well when taking on the challenge of the *Dundee Advertiser* as an ambitious 23-year-old. At the time of his death, John Leng & Co. was a successful business and major employer with a powerful, varied publishing base.

While John Leng was building his empire, William Thomson, the Dundee owner of a highly successful shipping line, started to diversify and took an interest in a local publishing company that was responsible for the *Dundee Courier and Argus*, as well as *The Weekly News*. In 1886 he bought out the company and established one of his sons, David Couper Thomson, born in Dundee in 1861, as the full controlling partner. Very soon the company became completely family run when another son, Frederick, and several nephews joined the firm. The ethos was that, family or not, they had to become full-time working partners, familiar with and working in all aspects of the business. There was to be no easy ride, no passengers on the gravy train.

Enthusiasm, hard work and financial solidarity quickly established W. & D.C. Thomson as the more dominant of the local publishing companies. David Couper Thomson had, by 1905, proved himself to be a shrewd businessman and the name of the company was changed to its present day form, D.C. Thomson, as he assumed control. To complete the change new premises were established in the now familiar red sandstone building in Albert Square and the move from its old North Lindsay Street site which it had occupied since 1872 was finalised in 1906.

The keen rivalry between Leng's and Thomson's was softened in 1906 when they entered an agreement to pool their businesses, with Thomson's taking the controlling interest. For a number of years the two companies operated side by side, each managing their own affairs, until 1926 when, following the devastating General Strike, it was agreed to merge the *Courier* and the *Advertiser* and John Leng & Co. ceased to exist.

In the ensuing years Thomson's has been responsible for publishing, at various times, more than 100 publications. It was after the end of the First World War, when staff returned from duty and the company found itself with an excess of capacity, that it made what turned out to be a masterstroke. It started producing children's story papers and tentatively launched the *Adventure*, which proved to be an immediate and massive success. Others quickly followed: *Rover*, *Wizard*, *Vanguard*, *Skipper* and *Hotspur* filling a niche in the tastes of British youth. The concept was further extended with the introduction of children's comics. The *Dandy* blazed the trail and was followed by the *Beano*, which is still popular with both kids and their dads!

David Thomson, the founder, died in 1954, but the company is still family run and family oriented. Its growth has been remarkable and it now distributes over 200 million magazines, periodicals, newspapers and comics annually throughout the British Isles. Although modern day progress has led to some diversification into television and the Internet, its core business has wisely remained unchanged. Old favourites including *The Courier*, *Evening Telegraph*, *Sunday Post*, *Beano*, *Dandy*, *My Weekly*, *The People's Friend* and many more are avidly read by vast numbers of Britons, their popularity undiminished, ensuring that Thomson's is still one of Britain's leading and largest publishers. Over the years the contribution of the journalistic industry to the economic health of Dundee has been immeasurable. Throughout constant industrial change

Leng and Thomson provided employment and a level of prosperity in the local community. They also provided a considerable amount of manpower in response to the demands of the First World War and once again on the outbreak of the Second World War in 1939.

At the onset of the First World War and in response to the call for volunteers the factories, mills and the publishing houses had emptied of young men determined to play their part. It is easy to understand that, particularly between Leng's and Thomson's, the rivalry between the respective businesses felt by their young staff would quickly dissolve as they bonded and developed a camaraderie in support of the common cause. The journalistic workplace must have been a strange environment as its young men left to take up arms. Machine rooms, engine departments, advertising, printing, circulation, caserooms, stereo and despatch, as well as the more glamorous vocations of reporter, journalist and writer were all depleted in the desire to teach 'The Hun' a lesson.

During the Second World War more than 250 of Thomson's staff enlisted in the British Armed Forces, including senior members of staff and the family. Several were decorated for their bravery but tragically nine lost their lives.

Unfortunately no accurate statistics are available for the number of men from Leng's and Thomson's that fought in the First World War, but it was probably more than 250. There are no indications either of the number of fatalities suffered by the two companies. Nevertheless, they were eager to fight and to operate as a band of brothers in the same battalion.

It is also easy to understand how the mood of the time would carry the doubters along, swept along on a tide of glory and optimism. Even the more educated, more intelligent of the journalism trade, the editorial staff, were not immune to the seduction of adventure and glory. The journalists and editorial staff of Thomson's and Leng's had set out for France in 1915, proud to be a part of the glorious Black Watch tradition. Bolstered by rhetoric, patriotism and a will to fight for honour, they were ready to pay the price. Sadly there was a price to pay and the grim reaper ensured that the offices of Thomson and Leng would never be the same. Familiar faces were missing from familiar desks and new faces coped

manfully with the loss of experienced staff. That close, happy bunch of editorial colleagues was sorely depleted.

One cold February day, just before the 4th Battalion left for France, nine journalist colleagues from John Leng & Co. had posed together for a memorable photograph. Resplendent in their full Black Watch uniforms covered by greatcoats, they looked determined and impressive; the Fighter Writers were on their way. Lance-Corporal Crosbie, Private Sellar, Private Joe Lee, Private John Nicholson, Private Anderson, Lance-Corporal Williamson, Private Hood, Lance-Corporal Addison and Lance-Corporal Linton Andrews enjoyed a camaraderie developed from working together as colleagues and friends. They were confident, as they set out on their great adventure, that they had the intelligence and ability to help each other, and to survive irrespective of the conditions. Remarkably, considering that the life expectancy for a solider fighting on the Western Front was measured in weeks, eight of the nine men in the photograph survived the war.

The Fighter Writers. From left to right, back row: Lance-Corporal Crosbie, Private Sellars, Private Joseph Lee, Private Nicholson, Private Anderson, Lance-Corporal Williamson. Front row: Private Hood, Lance-Corporal Addison, Lance-Corporal Andrews.

The only fatality was Private John (Jack) Beveridge Nicholson, killed by a sniper's bullet in July 1915 and buried in the military cemetery of Richebourt St Vaast. Nicholson, at 21, was the youngest of the group and worked with Joe Lee on *The People's Journal*. He was the son of the Revd T.B. Nicholson and, despite his tender years, he was regarded as a highly promising journalist. It was Nicholson and Andrews who started to send back reports on the war which attracted the attention of Lord Northcliffe. So impressed was he at the quality of the reports that he vowed, believing the reports to be the work of one man, to employ the reporter at the war's end. Nicholson also wrote poetry and was believed, particularly by Joe Lee, to be very talented. Sadly, only two poems have actually come into the public domain. Regrettably for Nicholson his full potential would never be realised, but his talent is underlined in a remarkable poem, centred on the Croix Rouge – a crossroads in Flanders. The crossroads was dominated by a Christ-like figure hanging from a cross, which was also the subject of a sketch and a poem by Joe Lee.

THE CRUCIFIX
by J.B. Nicholson

He hung there at the crossroads
On a Cross of rain-beat red,
And the nails that pierced His hands and feet
And the thorn-crown on His head
Showed awfully in the moonlight,
And it seemed that He was dead.

But I knelt beneath the Crucifix
And prayed with bowéd head,
And the nails that pierced His hands and feet
Fell out, all rusted red.
And shining in the moonlight
Was a gold crown on His head.

And He came from off the Crucifix,
He who had seemed dead,
And gently placed His pierced hand
In mine; and so He led
Me in the paling moonlight
To a place all bloody red.

'Here was a soldier's sacrifice',
He gently to me said,
'Here a man fell as was his meet,
For justice; and he bled
There in the ghostly moonlight
Till they said that he was dead.

But I saw him from yon Crucifix,
And I came with noiseless tread,
And took his heart and placed it
In a babe unborn instead.
And his soul sped in the moonlight,
And with God's in Heaven was wed.

And the babe shall be a hero,
Of that soldier's valour bred.
He shall live to lead his brothers,
But not in battle red:
He shall lead them to the sunlight,
When the Hell of War is dead'.

I awoke there at the crossroads
By the cross of rain-beat red

   * * * * *

And the nails that pierced His hands and feet
And the thorn-crown on His head
Showed awfully in the moonlight.

   * * * * *

But I knew He was not dead.

It was a beautiful, sensitive poem offering a tantalising glimpse of a poet with a mature, perceptive quality rare in one so young.

Linton Andrews survived the war, and indeed was the longest and the sole surviving member of the original volunteer group, serving only with the Black Watch. After volunteering, Andrews spent part of his training period in Dundee, billeted in a house where he fell in love with the owner's daughter. Before setting out for France he proposed to Gertie Douglas and she accepted. They were married during one of his leave periods in 1917, and after spending almost four years fighting on the Western Front, he was able to come home to her and they enjoyed a long and happy married life. True to his word, Lord Northcliffe employed the sole surviving war correspondent, and Andrews joined the *Daily Mail* at the war's end. In 1923 he moved to the *Leeds Mercury* as editor and 16 years later, when it merged with the *Yorkshire Post*, he was again appointed editor. In journalistic circles he adopted a high profile, serving at various times as President of the Editor's Guild, President of the Institute of Journalists and Chairman of the Press Council, and he was knighted for his services. Despite his workload he still found time to write two books, *The Haunting Years*, describing his wartime experiences, and *The Autobiography of a Journalist*. Sir Linton Andrews, Joe Lee's closest friend, had done more than his share and deserved the success and happiness which the post-war years brought.

Private J.M. Hood was promoted to lieutenant, serving eventually with the Machine Gun Corps. He was captured by the Germans and remarkably ended up, for a spell, in Carlsruhe prisoner of war camp with Joe Lee. A photograph of the two men, taken at Carlsruhe, was published in the *Dundee Advertiser* while they were incarcerated.

Lance-Corporal Willie Addison was promoted to lieutenant, survived the war, and emigrated to South Africa where he edited a newspaper in Johannesburg. He eventually became the Speaker of the Legislative Assembly of Southern Rhodesia.

Private Sellar (Sellars in the photograph) was the man who, while on recruitment duty, had to ask Joe Lee his age and was told to mind his own business. After the war R.J.B. Sellar remained in journalism and wrote, in 1952, a very succinct tribute to Joe Lee in the *Scots Magazine*.

Private Willie Anderson, who later joined the Signallers, Lance-Corporal Williamson and Lance-Corporal Crosbie also returned to Dundee at the war's end.

The 'Nine Just Men' or 'Band of Brothers' were not of course the only journalistic staff who enlisted and went to the Western Front to fight; some paid the ultimate price, others were wounded. Private Skerry, who had been the foreign sub-editor on the *Dundee Advertiser* and indeed had been responsible for collating and reporting the news of the outbreak of the war for the paper, was killed at the Battle of Loos in 1915. During the battle the 4th Battalion of the Black Watch, after suffering horrendous casualties, started to move back and Skerry fell back with them. Suddenly, and inexplicably, he stopped, turned to face the enemy and charged the Germans. His colleagues saw him cut down, with no hope of survival; a moment of madness, bravery, pride – who knows, perhaps a combination of all three.

'Pal' Stirton, called Pal because he couldn't remember names and called everyone 'Pal', also from the *Dundee Advertiser*, once asked Andrews to promise him that, if he were killed in action, he would not be buried by the side of the road. He said 'If you do I will hear the Black Watch boys marching to the trenches and I'll be sore at heart that I can't come with them,' – camaraderie indeed, and a real love for the regiment. Stirton was also killed at Loos. Another colleague, Dave Chapman, was also a victim of that horrendous battle.

In one of the Black Watch's earlier battles at Festubert, another editorial colleague, a promising singer called Chick Wallace, was killed, and Jimmy Scott and R. Spark were badly wounded. Later in the war, in July 1917, D. Hunter, a colleague who had featured in those early happy training days in Dundee, also died. No wonder then that when the survivors returned there were several familiar faces missing from the offices of Thomson's and Leng's.

The price had been severe, and the big adventure had been costly. The original group of nine Fighter Writers, photographed for posterity before setting out for the war, miraculously lost only one colleague, but of the total group of about 18 editorial staff who set out for glory, five died, five were wounded and two became prisoners of war.

CHAPTER SEVEN

New Beginnings

C HASTENED by his wartime experiences, and saddened by the loss
of friends and colleagues, Lee realised that things could never be the
same again. At the age of 42 he was at a crossroads in his life. Much
respected, almost revered in Dundee, he enjoyed for a period the comfort
of being at home and getting to know his nieces, Chrissie and Kathleen.
There was still the matter of his career to pursue and he intended writing
a book about his incarceration at Carlsruhe. However, there was another
matter, of greater importance, which occupied his mind – Dorothy Barrie.
Despite his first disastrous attempt to impress her over lunch in London
while he was on leave, they had kept in touch. She was still in London at
the Royal Academy, studying music, and he was back in Dundee
pondering which road to take to rebuild his life.

His books of war poetry, *Ballads of Battle* and *Work-a-day Warriors,*
had attracted considerable attention and his poems and sketches had
enthralled a wider audience, through mainstream British publications
and others in America and Canada. His celebrity was such that if he had
been single-minded or ambitious he could certainly have used his fame to
his advantage. Spurning a golden opportunity to capitalise on his success,
he followed his heart and made the decision that guaranteed his
happiness for the rest of his life: he moved to London to be near Dorothy.

As a young man in his twenties, he had worked in newspapers in
London and did know his way around. For a time he found work as a
reporter and attended trials at the Old Bailey, making sketches of the
participants. In his spare time he once again attended the Slade School of

Chrissie Blackwood, older sister to Kathleen, Joe Lee's niece and the recipient of Joe's letter from the trenches in 1917. Chrissie died in 2001 in her 92nd year.

Art, which was now, along with Dorothy, his overriding passion. It was a busy time, working for the newspaper, attending art classes and courting Dorothy. His book *A Captive at Carlsruhe* was published and was selling steadily and he did now and again manage to visit Dundee.

It was on one such visit in 1922 that he wrote, on the train from King's Cross to Dundee, his last significant poem 'A Northern Town'. The poem, his first for some considerable time, showed that his poetic talents had not diminished. He had survived the devastating effects of the war and prisoner of war camp, so one could forgive him for being sentimental or emotional in his recollection. However, as ever he is focused and clear. He recalls warm sunny days, going barefoot in the streets, winter days watching the shivering coughing mill workers hurrying to work, women in shawls, giant looms whirring and the wailing of the factory whistles through births, marriages and funerals. He writes of playing truant and bird nesting and of a different wailing when the schoolmaster punished him for truancy. The exotic and sordid side of a sea-faring town is beautifully illustrated:

> But to-day – There are the wharves to haunt where the great clippers
>   tethered
> And sun tanned seaman lolled
> O'er the ships side, with rings hung in their ears
> And ocean in their eyes
> And money in their belts
> So that strange women lay at the gates in wait
> And in the secret houses orgies were
> And sometimes a wild screaming woke the night
> When knives were drawn.

Lee writes of watching the whaling fleets sail out to sea and return with their cargo, and sometimes catching sight of a chained bear cub on deck. Hired cabs arrived to collect whalers and their wives, children or sweethearts and their sea chests and souvenirs, and Lee remembers the stench of whale around the narrow streets, for weeks after the return of the fleet. Sometimes the streets would be blocked by horses pulling huge loads up steep inclines and at other times the streets would be filled with 'clattering wagons and clanging cars'. Nethergate thronged with jostling crowds and lovers enjoyed the twilight on the Esplanade. The weekend, as ever, it seems, ended in drunken revelry. Lee recalls a sun-tanned tribe of tinkers with their jangling pots and pans and skirling pipes, bawling market tradesmen, and shouting showmen and their roundabouts. St Mary's Old Town bell would ring at 10pm, reminding Lee and his friends to hurry home. One can imagine that for a young boy, particularly an intelligent boy, these sights would create a lasting impression.

This, once again, was the real Dundee, the town of his boyhood. Even after his wartime experiences he was able to recapture the poetic voice that had described Dundee in such affectionate detail in *Tales O' Our Town*. In 1910, for that publication, he wrote in the last verse of his poem 'The Nethergate':

> And when at last it comes to me
> To quietly lay me doon and dee,
> And sinfu' I, perchance make bold
> To venture nigh to Streets of Gold;
> As at the unbarred Heavens I wait,
> I'll think on kindly Nethergate!

In 1922 he concluded *A Northern Town* with:

> Old town, old stones, old streets, old memories
> It is good to return to you in life and dream
> It were good to return to you in death and dream.

His wish, to return to Dundee before he died, would be granted.

Apart from 'A Northern Town', after the First World War Lee wrote very little poetry. He switched his attention to sketching and painting, and he only wrote poetry for friends or special occasions. An excellent example is an obituary poem dedicated to Dundee man Frank Sharp, who died in November 1923 and moved Lee to take up his pen. Sharp was a popular music teacher who specialised in teaching children, not only to sing but also to enjoy music. He organised concerts for massed choirs which Joe's sister Kate had participated in and was well known to Joe and his brother Herman. Lee's simple tribute is warm and heartfelt.

FRANK SHARP

> He is not dead –
> Just forward on the way,
> With high-flung and defiant head,
> On this autumnal day.

He is not dead –
Only a farewell flung;
Not the last word is said,
Nor the last song sung.

He is not dead –
Still is the clear voice ringing;
Only with swift foot sped
To where – are children singing!

＊ ＊ ＊ ＊ ＊

Working in London, Joe Lee was kept busy. He attended the Old Bailey to report on the Edith Thompson and Frederick Bywaters murder trial of December 1922. Edith Thompson, aged 28, was accused of inciting her young lover, Frederick Bywaters, aged 20, to murder her husband. She had written Bywaters letters in which she had hinted at murder, suggesting that she had, on one occasion, put the shattered glass from a light bulb into his food, and when that had failed she had started to explore the possibilities of poisons. Furthermore she told Bywaters that she wanted him to be jealous of her husband, so jealous that he might do something desperate. When the Thompsons returned from a London theatre visit, Bywaters emerged from the shadows and stabbed Percy Thompson. As he lay dying, Edith called for help. After her husband died she gave Bywaters's name to the police. When the case opened at the Old Bailey, Edith Thompson was advised by her counsel not to take the stand, but she ignored his advice and was severely mauled during the cross-examination. In summing up, the judge advised the jury that they were trying a 'vulgar common crime' and described Edith Thompson's letters as 'full of the outpourings of a silly but at the same time wicked affection'.

Lee remembers the case as being more tense and dramatic than any Greek tragedy or Shakespearean play, with two hapless human beings striving to disentangle themselves from a web of evil. As he closely observed Edith Thompson during his sketching, he noticed her pallor and her futile attempts to moisten lips parched with terror. It was, he said, a sight that he would never forget; it reminded him of the Roman soldiers placing vinegar onto a sponge and giving it to our dying Lord. Thompson's sister stood up in court and pleaded for her, and her mother, overcome with tension, fainted and had to be carried from the court. Lee's keen eye spotted a relative of Bywaters tap on the glass screen with a coin to attract his attention and noticed a brave attempt at a smile from the doomed youth as he was led from the court.

Although Bywaters defended Thompson to the end, claiming that she had done nothing to incite him to kill her husband, they were both found guilty of murder. At the same hour on 9 January 1923 Bywaters was hanged at Pentonville Prison and Thompson at Holloway.

Another famous trial of the period, during which Lee enjoyed the sparring and the posturing, was the Russell paternity case. The performances of the two barristers were particularly memorable. Sir John Simon was described by Lee as cold and as impervious as an iceberg, while Patrick Hastings was as explosive and fiery as a volcano. Mrs Russell had gone to a ball with a male friend and when he brought her back to her flat she claimed that she had lost her key. Not wishing to wake her husband she decided, as she put it, to do the 'obvious thing' and returned to the flat of her male companion, where she spent the night. This was the basis of the paternity case. Lee noted the way that Sir John suddenly pulled his gown on to his shoulder and snapped, 'Tell me, Mrs Russell, did you really lose that key?' 'It would appear so,' she answered tamely. 'Madam, that is not an answer to my question', he retorted, then after a pause, said 'Tell me, Mrs Russell, did you ever find that key?' 'No.' she replied. Sir John turned to the jury with a dramatic shrug. 'She did what she thought was the obvious thing.'

This was an enjoyable time in Lee's life. He had the opportunity to attend high-profile court cases, sketching the scenes and reporting back, while at the same time fitting in art lessons and wooing Dorothy. Dorothy had actually finished her violin tuition and had been offered and taken a teaching position at the Royal Academy of Music. Sadly, in 1923 her mother was taken seriously ill and she had to return to Dundee to help look after her and run the household. Joe was a great comfort to her at that time, and when he asked for her hand in marriage she readily agreed. The engagement, 'Scottish Poet-Artist's Engagement To Marry Dundee

Dorothy Barrie,
Britain's leading
viola player, *c.*1920

Lady Musician' was announced in the local newspapers and the wedding was fixed for 7 January 1924. The couple's many friends were delighted; it truly was a fairy story. Joseph Lee, aged 48, had wooed and won the young lady of 24 whom he had sketched when as a little girl of 12 she had won a music competition. Now she was about to become his wife.

Dorothy was the youngest child of five and the only child in the family with musical ability. Her father, George Barrie, was himself a musician and naturally took a keen interest in Dorothy, encouraging and helping her develop her potential. Her first school, the Morgan Academy, realised that they had a special talent on their hands and were accommodating about the more mundane aspects of schoolwork. For example, they were not too insistent on her completing projects or homework if she would play the piano or violin, or sing at concerts. Her father was extremely proud of her ability, particularly when she was able to perform with him and his fellow musicians.

It was believed that she had potential worth nurturing, and she was enrolled as a student at the Royal Academy of Music in London. However, despite eight years of hard work, hoping to make the grade as a concert violinist or at least become a member of a leading orchestra, it was not to be. At least not just yet. The Royal Academy had a world-wide reputation and attracted aspiring talented youngsters from all over the globe; competition was extremely fierce. Dorothy was certainly talented, but she hadn't quite got that extra edge; nevertheless the Academy offered her a teaching role so they must have been impressed.

When Dorothy was called back to Dundee to nurse her mother, she was expected to participate in running the household, which was completely foreign to her. Her studies and concentrated, focused work had resulted in only a passing acquaintance with domesticity – she couldn't cook! Kathleen Blackwood remembers that one of Dorothy's sisters, who was a domestic science teacher in a Dundee school, came to her rescue. Dorothy applied herself in the kitchen with the same determination with which she had tackled her musical career; very soon she was an accomplished cook and Joe Lee would remain forever grateful to his sister-in-law. Sadly Dorothy's mother did not live long enough to see her daughter married at Fairmuir Parish Church, Dundee, on 7 January 1924.

Joe and Dorothy's wedding was a grand affair, prompting a local newspaper headline 'Wedding – Talented Musician and Poet-Artist'. The article recounted in some detail the decoration of the church and the guests' outfits.

The church was decorated with lilies and palms and Dorothy entered

SCOTTISH POET-ARTIST'S ENGAGEMENT.

To Marry Dundee Lady Musician.

Dundee, Saturday.

The large circle of friends of Mr Joseph J. Lee, the well-known soldier-poet and artist, will be pleased to know of his engagement and approaching marriage.

A member of the 4th Black Watch, and later commissioned in the K.R.R., "Joe," as he was popularly known, was taken prisoner in November, 1917.

Previous to being taken prisoner he had written poems with sketches while in the trenches, and just after he was captured his book "Work-a-Day Warriors," was published.

His bride is Miss Dorothy H. Barrie, a well-known Dundee lady, with rare musical talent as a violinist. Miss Barrie studied music in the London Royal Academy for eight years, and since coming home, about a year ago, has given several private recitals. The wedding, it is understood, will take place early in January.

The announcement that appeared in the Dundee papers on the engagement of Joe Lee to Dorothy Barrie.

wearing a gown of white crêpe de chine interwoven with silver. Her veil of draped white net was held in place by a decoration of bride's blossom and her bouquet was white lilac and white carnations. There were three bridesmaids, including Chrissie Blackwood, Joe's first niece, who wore a little frock of white net over white satin and carried a bouquet of anemones. Joe's sister Kate, the mother of Chrissie and Kathleen, wore a soft shade of blue velvet with a black picture hat trimmed with blue. Kathleen, aged eight, accompanied her mother in a cream lace frock over very pale pink. Joe's brother Herman and his wife Grace, dressed in mole coloured velvet with a matching hat and a seal coat, completed the Lee family party. Mole, seal and skunk fur were indicative of the fashion of the time, while the description printed in the newspaper of the colour of one lady's attire as 'nigger brown', would today be considered wholly inappropriate. When the couple left for their honeymoon Dorothy, the new Mrs Lee, wore a suit of grey jacquard trimmed with mole fur and a hat of light russet shade. A coat of grey jacquard trimmed with mole completed her going away outfit.

Joe Lee was a happy man, a very happy man. At an age when most men would have believed that love had passed them by he had found a happiness that would bring him stability. Shortly after their honeymoon the couple decided that their future lay in London and they found a small semi-detached house in Epsom. Dorothy had numerous contacts in the music field and wished to pursue her career, while Joe had many well-established contacts in the field of journalism. Following her failure to reach the heights as a violinist, Dorothy embarked on a career change and elected to study the viola under the renowned and much-respected Lionel Tertis.

Tertis, born in West Hartlepool in 1876, had studied the violin in Leipzig, and had become the world's leading viola player. He was much in demand in Europe and America. Although the viola was not a particularly popular instrument, Tertis's talent and unique skills seduced later composers, such as Vaughan Williams and Walton, into writing pieces especially for him. Tertis had developed the unique ability to extract from the viola a stronger and more intense tone, and by designing a larger instrument he was able to produce an even richer, more powerful effect.

Dorothy and Joe took every opportunity to watch Tertis perform in concert and she was very fortunate to have lessons on a one-to-one basis from the maestro. Years later, on 23 February 1937, they attended a concert to celebrate Tertis's 60th birthday and were surprised to read in the *Daily Telegraph* a few days later that Tertis had announced his retirement due to the onset of rheumatism. He had decided that his affliction was impairing his ability to play to his own high standards and he was not prepared to play in public again. The Lees admired his courage, and Dorothy wrote to him respecting his decision but expressing the hope that he would continue to give her lessons. Tertis, in fact, started to teach more and more, promoting the viola at every opportunity, and he did still manage to play on special occasions. He took the opportunity to write a book, *Beauty of Tone in String Playing*,

COWDRAY HALL
Iᴀ HENRIETTA STREET
W.ɪ

———

An

Invitation Recital

of

PIANO QUARTETS

by

ELSIE OWEN
(Violin)

DOROTHY LEE
(Viola)

LILY PHILLIPS
(Cello)

ALAN RICHARDSON
(Pianoforte)

Thursday, March 2nd
at 8.30

which was published in 1938, and on his 90th birthday EMI issued an LP of his work. Lionel Tertis was made a CBE in 1950 and died in 1975 at the grand old age of 98. Dorothy could not have been in better hands when she embarked on her viola lessons in the 1920s.

A programme for one of Dorothy's concerts.

Joe continued to study art at the Slade, despite accepting a position as sub-editor on the *News Chronicle*. The newly-weds found that their lives were full and demanding, and populated with an ever-increasing circle of friends and associates.

Dorothy's talent flourished on the viola, and during her time studying with Lionel Tertis she joined a quartet of lady musicians. Shortly afterwards she also found time to join an orchestra. During this period Lee too was making a name for himself with pencil, paint and brush. Some of his works received critical acclaim from other painters and experienced critics. His tutor at the Slade was a Professor Tonks.

Professor Henry Tonks was one of the most influential figures in the art world during the first half of the 20th century. He had taken over as head of the Slade in 1918 and quickly established the Slade style, which by the time of his death in 1937 had sadly become unfashionable. Nevertheless Stanley Spencer was just one of the many talented painters to have benefited from his tutorage. Tonks was himself a highly regarded artist and in 1936 the Tate Gallery held an exhibition of his works, which Tonks later bequeathed to the Slade. Although Lee's description of him is far from flattering: 'a tall austere man – a long grey shadow stripped for a fight – a herring gutted man, with the head of an ancient Roman – a Julius Caesar in trousers instead of a toga', he was extremely fond of him and described his year at the Slade under Tonks as among the happiest memories of his time in London. Tonks does appear to have been a terrifying sight – Lee recalls that one lady artist wrote in her autobiography that so alarmed was she at the apparition of Tonks, who appeared to be nine feet tall, that she fled the Slade and enlisted at the Westminster School of Art instead.

Apparition or not, Tonks had an excellent reputation and taught, as Lee explained, in epigram. He implored his students to draw like scientists. Earlier in his life he had been a surgeon and would dissect a poor drawing with a wit as sharp as a scalpel, writing humorous critical comments in the margins of pupil's works.

However, he clearly took a shine to Joe Lee, who was surprised and delighted on one occasion when Tonks, in the middle of writing pencilled comments on a drawing of Lee's, suddenly said 'I would like you to come to dinner in my studios some Saturday evening, George Moore and Wilson Steer are sure to blow in – what Saturday could you come?' Lee immediately replied 'This Saturday'. Tonks said 'Come early, I want to show you some of my pictures and I am a bit tired of Moore's criticism of my work.' During dinner that Saturday night Tonks confided that he wondered whether his life, totally dedicated to art, had been a selfish one, but explained 'I have no other credo. I have even thought of having myself chained to the railings of Hyde Park and calling to all that pass by, come and be saved by the beneficent power of art.' Later that night George Moore and Wilson Steer and others did indeed blow in. Tonks had introduced Lee into the magic circle of the famous studios, the Vale, which will be familiar to all readers of George Moore.

Joe Lee, during his time as reporter and journalist in Dundee and London, and as an artist in London, came into contact with many famous figures of the period, many of whose work and acclaim has lasted and will last for as long as art and literature are enjoyed. Many of these influences and acquaintances will be looked at more closely in a later chapter.

These were busy days for Joe Lee – studying at the Slade in the morning and then devoting the rest of the day and early evening to journalism made life hectic. Nevertheless, Joe and Dorothy were extremely happy. Despite their great circle of friends and contacts they remained modest and well balanced. They did give private parties, concerts, recitals and so on for friends, but never sought celebrity, fame or publicity. Joe's love of art, poetry, books and music was entirely compatible with Dorothy's cultural tastes and he often called for her opinion or comment when he wanted a critical assessment that he could trust. They were comfortable in each other's company and cherished their private moments together. One cold November day in 1926 Joe was reading by the fire while Dorothy was curled up asleep on the couch. Joe studied her with his artist's eye, noting how beautiful she looked. Fascinated by her face, he decided to go and get his sketchbook. However, thinking better of it he resisted the urge, believing that it was wrong to sketch her without her knowledge.

Some days Joe would wave Dorothy off to London for rehearsals with the quartet, then go for a walk around the village before setting off for London and Fleet Street and work. However, when Dot was not due in London herself, she would drive Joe to the station at Epsom to catch the London train and then pick him up later that night. As Joe's working day usually started in the afternoons they did manage to spend some time together. In the cold days of winter Joe liked it when Dorothy moved into his study to practice, to keep warm and to share his company while he studied or wrote his journals. They enjoyed this quiet routine in otherwise very busy lives.

The couple particularly enjoyed going to London to see concerts together and often Dorothy would drive. Joe would try to visit the art galleries, exhibitions, and museums, and would occasionally review a show or exhibition for the newspaper. In March 1927 he visited the Bond Street Art Gallery to see a new exhibit, Stanley Spencer's *The Last Resurrection*. It was particularly resonant for Lee, because as he gazed at the newly acclaimed masterpiece he thought back to the times that he had enjoyed with Spencer, when they had studied together at the Slade. Stanley Spencer was now making a name for himself.

Dorothy's musical quartet found themselves increasingly in demand and she would get nervous before a performance and would occasionally indulge in what Joe called a 'wee draught' to settle her nerves. Regrettably, after a while Dorothy began to find the travelling to London for regular rehearsals very tiring, and despite the quartet's success, which included radio broadcasts as well as numerous concert appearances, she resigned.

Having a little time on her hands at last enabled Dorothy to help Joe with his work sometimes, and he did value her usually forthright and honest opinions. Once during a literary discussion with him she said 'Jane Austen's work is as good as a dose of bromide to me.' No beating about the bush there.

Occasionally members of the Lee family would venture out of Scotland and come to stay with them. Nelly came in the summer of 1936 and they visited Canterbury, enjoying lunch at Reigate and then having coffee, ham and chicken sandwiches in a Canterbury pub.

Nelly was followed by niece Kathleen Blackwood, who came to stay with them in the autumn of 1936. Kathleen ostensibly came to London to have six months of further music lessons in preparation for her London Royal Academy of Music examination. It was a very happy time for all of them, with music being the focal point.

Sometimes the daily routine of newspaper duties frustrated Joe, as this description of one day graphically illustrates. He comments: 'Seven hours, seven columns of Welsh news – how I weary of it'. Nevertheless home life was happy, with the house full of music as Kathleen played Bach and Dot rehearsed. Dorothy and Kathleen would often drive up to London for a concert or lessons and Joe would meet them for coffee and chocolate at a favourite little Italian café near the Law Courts if they had been to a Beecham Concert at Queen's Hall. Such was their enthusiasm for the concerts that Dorothy would not be deterred no matter what the weather.

The Lee's home in Epsom, Surrey.

Once Joe tried to stop them leaving in Dot's little car when a thunderstorm was imminent and the forecast threatened snow. They set off despite his concerns, enjoyed the concert and returned home safely to a relieved Joe.

Even now, more than 65 years later, Kathleen Blackwood still remembers visiting her Uncle Joe and Auntie Dorothy at their house in Epsom. They did appear to have an idyllic lifestyle. Joe was very fond of the motor car but neither drove it nor wanted to, although he enjoyed having Dorothy drive him around. They would make frequent trips into Epsom for light shopping, stopping for coffee and a piece of Fortnum & Mason's Iced Walnut Cake. Many times when he had free mornings they would drive to the Downs or visit other little villages, enjoying a flask of coffee in the car or dropping into a small café. Days off would be filled with trips to Reigate or Leatherhead, Crawley, Horsham Hunt or Partridge Green, with stops at quaint cafes for sandwiches or toasted teacakes. At other times Joe would immerse himself in his study among his vast collection of books. Sundays were blissfully peaceful: tea, toast, and *The Sunday Times,* and later Dorothy would practice while Joe peeled potatoes. After lunch they would often drive into London to go to a concert.

Journalistically the 1930s was not too challenging until the later years. The death of King George V in 1936, however, was a particularly difficult time. Lee recalls that the long drawn-out passing of the King created enormous difficulties for the newspaper. Every night the paper had to be made up virtually in duplicate, in case the King should die. The staff had to put in extra work, and Joe once again responded with the unflappable character that had stood him in good stead throughout his life.

Joe Lee's great-niece, Kathleen Blackwood, eloquently summarised their tastes in the late 1930s. She said of her uncle and aunt:

> They loved the gentle rolling landscapes, the quiet country lanes and the tiny hidden villages. They loved the music of Elgar, Delius and Vaughan Williams and the paintings of Constable. They loved birdsong and the sound of a dimpling brook and the moonlight and sunrise and beauty and peace.

However, in October 1938 Dorothy received a boost when she was approached by Kathleen Riddick, the conductor of the London Women's String Orchestra, and invited to join them for rehearsals. Welcoming their approach and the opportunity to get back into formal music, Dorothy accepted the invitation and very quickly impressed Kathleen Riddick, who described Dorothy as the best instrumentalist in the orchestra and appointed her lead viola. On her birthday, 11 November, Joe gave her a cheque for a new dress, but more importantly for Dorothy, he bought her *The Oxford Companion to Music*.

The pride Joe felt for her is very evident, but perhaps he displayed a little male chauvinism when in the concert programme dated Sunday 5 February 1939, for a performance at the Conway Hall in Holborn, he ringed Dorothy's name and wrote 'Joseph Lee's wife' next to it.

In early February 1939 Joe recalled a concert that was more memorable for the 'vile' coloured publicity poster than for the artist, who would nevertheless go on to make a considerable impact in the world of classical music. The poster proclaimed 'YEHUDI MENUHEN…The Prodigy of Yesterday – The Genius of Today.' This was exactly the kind of self-proclaimed publicity that Lee found distasteful.

Dorothy enjoyed considerable success with her new orchestra, which culminated in them being introduced to a gramophone company with the

PRICE TWOPENCE.

SOUTH PLACE SUNDAY CONCERT SOCIETY.
SOUTH PLACE SUNDAY CONCERTS
(CHAMBER MUSIC)
ALFRED J. CLEMENTS, ORGANISER AND HONORARY SECRETARY FROM 1887 TO 1958.
CONWAY HALL, Red Lion Square, Holborn, W.C.1.
SEVENTEENTH CONCERT OF THE FIFTY-THIRD SEASON (1326th CONCERT).

Sunday, 5th February, 1939, at 6.30 p.m.   Doors open at 6.10

I. THE LONDON WOMEN'S STRING ORCHESTRA :

Conductor - KATHLEEN RIDDICK

First Violins :	*Second Violins :*	*Violoncellos :*
VERA KANTROVITCH (Leader)	JEAN LE FEVRE	EDITH LAKE
HILDA PARRY	SYLVIA MORRIS	HILDEGARD ARNOLD
QUEENIE DYER	ESTHER RIXON	BARBARA LOYNES
DOROTHY EVERITT	MIRIAM FISHBEIN	
DOROTHY MASSEY	*Violas :*	*Double Basses :*
MONICA VINCENT	DOROTHY LEE	DORIS GREENISH
	FRANCES HOWE	MARGARET FAIRFAX
	PHILLIS TATE	

Joseph Lee's wife → [DOROTHY LEE]

1. SUITE ... ... *Rameau, arr. R. Temple Savage.*
   I. L'Egyptienne. II. Menuet. III. Rondo "Les Tendres Plaintes." IV. Rigaudon. V. Two Gigues en Rondeaux.

2. SONGS ... (a) Wehmut   (b) Lachen und Weinen   *Schubert (1797-1828)*
              (c) Es träumte mir   (d) Meine Liebe ist Grün   *Brahms (1833-1897)*
   MICHAEL HEAD (to his own accompaniment).

(a) WEHMUT

When through the woods and fields I roam,
A joy, a pain, upon me come
And pierce my troubled breast ;
A joy, a pain, upon me press
In Spring's full tide of loveliness,
When all seems bright and blest.
For trees that wave with music soft,
And clouds that heavenward tower aloft,
And even Man, so dearly bound
To earthly beauty shining round,
Dissolving, pass away.
          The Hon. Rollo Russell.

(b) LACHEN UND WEINEN

Laughter and tears are the changing
moods of love. At evening I am sad, but at
dawn I awaken with happiness. I do not
know why, . . . only my heart knows the
reason.

(c) ES TRAUMTE MIR

I dreamed at night that I was dear to thee,
But all too late came the morning gleam ;
For ere I awakened, too well I knew
It was a dream.

(d) MEINE LIEBE IST GRÜN

Like a blossoming lilac my love is fair,
Like a sunbeam proudly she gloweth ;
Sweet odours it makes in the lilac bush,
And lo ! into flower it bloweth.

And my soul has the plumes of a nightingale,
Mid odourous blossoms it wingeth,
Entranced by the bliss that on all is poured,
With joy o'erflowing it singeth.

3. ... ... (a) Two Aquarelles ... ... *Delius (1863-1934)*
                   (b) Romance in C ... ... *Sibelius (b. 1865)*
                   (c) Adagio e Giga ... ... *Galuppi, arr. Esposito*

4. CONCERTO IN D, Op. 21, for Pianoforte and String Orchestra ... ... *Haydn (1732-1809)*
   I. Vivace. II. Un poco Adagio. III. Rondo all'Ungherese ; Allegro assai.
   First time at these Concerts.
   MICHAEL HEAD and THE LONDON WOMEN'S STRING ORCHESTRA.

INTERVAL FOR SILVER COLLECTION.

5. SONGS ... ... (a) Green Rain   (b) The King of China's Daughter }
                 (c) Fallen Veils   (d) Mamble   } *Michael Head*
   THE COMPOSER, to his own accompaniment.

(a) GREEN RAIN.

Into the scented woods we'll go
And see the blackthorn swim in snow.
High above in the budding leaves,
A brooding dove awakes and grieves ;
The glades with mingled music stir
And wildly laughs the woodpecker.
When blackthorn petals pearl the breeze,
There are the twisted hawthorn trees
Thick set with buds, as clear and pale
As golden water or green hail,
As if a storm of rain had stood
Enchanted in the thorny wood.

And, hearing fairy voices call,
Hung poised, forgetting how to fall.
                    Mary Webb.
(From Poems and the Spring of Joy.
                    Jonathan Cape)

(b) THE KING OF CHINA'S DAUGHTER.

The King of China's daughter,
She never would love me
Though I hung my cap and bells upon
Her nutmeg tree.
For oranges and lemons,
The stars in bright blue air,

(I stole them long ago, my dear)
Were dangling there.
The Moon did give me silver pence,
The Sun did give me gold,
And both together softly blew
And made my porridge cold ;
But the King of China's daughter
Pretended not to see
When I hung my cap and bells upon
Her nutmeg tree.
                    Edith Sitwell.
          (By permission of the author).

Joe Lee has encircled Dorothy's name on this concert programme and written 'Joseph Lee's wife'.

intention of making a record. Sadly, following the bereavement of one of the leaders of the orchestra it was unable to continue and regrettably disbanded. Dorothy joined another quartet and continued to play in concerts and recitals, but although she was widely regarded as Britain's leading female viola player, further progress and recognition would be halted by the impending war. But for the time being her days were full of musical commitments, and when Joe was taken ill during June 1939 she needed help looking after him, so Herman's wife Grace came down from Dundee to the rescue.

Alas, the couple's idyllic lifestyle was soon to come to an abrupt end. For Joe Lee the memories of a tragic and devastating war had faded, but they were soon to be reawakened. Once again in his lifetime the clouds of war were gathering across Europe.

CHAPTER EIGHT

The Second World War

AT the end of the First World War the 1919 Treaty of Versailles imposed a number of conditions on the defeated Germany and also created a new state, Czechoslovakia, which included the Sudetenland, a region containing almost four million German-speaking inhabitants. An ambitious militant activist, Adolf Hitler, declared in his 1924 book *Mein Kampf* that he would restore the might of Germany and tear up the Treaty of Versailles, by force if necessary. Gradually and stealthily he pursued his ambitions and when he became Chancellor of Germany in 1933 he immediately recognised that the time was ripe for action. He instigated a massive rearmament programme, withdrew Germany from the League of Nations, reoccupied the demilitarised Rheinland buffer zone with France, sent military aid to Franco fighting the Spanish Civil War and pressurised Austria into a union with the German Reich. Unrest in the Sudetenland gave him the excuse he needed; Hitler threatened military action against Czechoslovakia if it refused to hand over the Sudetenland to Germany. Although both France and the Soviet Union had treaties agreeing to come to Czechoslovakia's aid in time of war, the dispute was referred to Britain.

Hitler appeared to be prepared for war, while the Allies were not united and had little stomach for a fight. Neville Chamberlain, the British Prime Minister, negotiated the sacrifice of the Sudetenland to Germany. Although Chamberlain told the British people that the Munich Agreement was 'Peace with honour', and said that Britain and Germany had pledged never to go to war again, it was soon to be seen as a shameful, naïve exercise in appeasement. Hitler, spurred on by the demonstration of weakness by the Allies, annexed the whole of Czechoslovakia within six months of his meeting with Chamberlain. Certain now of his enemy's weakness, Hitler, believing the German Reich to be unstoppable, invaded Poland on 1 September 1939 after offering Britain an alliance, which was rejected. On 3 September Britain and France declared war on Germany, barely 21 years after the end of the calamitous conflict of the First World War. The same protagonists were once again in opposition.

The significant difference between the two wars was that death was now no longer restricted to armies fighting hundreds of miles away from home on some far-flung foreign field. The advent of air power, with fighters, bombers and the pilotless German V1 and V2 rockets, meant that major cities could be destroyed and civilians killed by an unseen enemy. Strategically, of course, the priority was to destroy important installations – ports, docks, railways and munitions factories – rather than to deliberately harm civilians. The early months of the war suggested little of the horrors to come. While Hitler was scheming and posturing, war was regarded by most good judges as inevitable.

In January 1939 the British Government launched an appeal for volunteers to respond to the call to National Service, stressing that the intention was to sue for peace, not war. The Lord Privy Seal's office issued three public information leaflets in July 1939, entitled 'Some Things You Should Know If War Should Come', 'Your Gas Mask and Evacuation,' and 'Why And How', to help prepare the British people for a war. The newspapers had been warning of the inevitability of war and Germany's invasion of Poland was the last straw. For Joe Lee at the *News Chronicle* it was very much *déja vu*. His editorial experience of the build-up to the First World War had made him wise to the machinations of international politics. Deadlines and headlines, late working, interpreting statements and writing editorials kept him busy as events progressed.

The public was psychologically prepared for conflict and when it came the early weeks brought little hardship to the civilian population. However, the impact of the war gradually began to have an effect on daily lives. Germany, recognising Britain's dependence on imported food, had successfully launched a submarine campaign, sinking many cargo ships laden with meat, sugar, fruit and wheat. Very soon food supplies started to dwindle and National Registration commenced in late September 1939, requiring everyone to have an identity card and ration book. Petrol rationing also began in 1939, and private car users were given a very meagre allowance, which was abandoned altogether in 1942. Germany's submarine strategy led to the implementation of food rationing on 8 January 1940. In the first phase a weekly allowance of four ounces of butter, four ounces of bacon or ham and 12 ounces of sugar was permitted per person, on the production of the ration book, at the shop where the customer was registered, in exchange for the related coupons. Shopping became a frustrating experience, since you had to go to different shops for bread, meat and vegetables, and queue in each to exchange coupons for small amounts of food. Often people would queue for a long time, only to be turned away because there was nothing left. As the weeks went by rationing was extended to include more foodstuffs, such as cheese, tea and eggs, while fruit such as grapes, bananas and oranges became scarce in most households.

To combat shortages the government launched a 'Dig for Victory' campaign encouraging the public to grow their own vegetables. Very soon every available space, no matter how small, was being used to grow potatoes, beans and cabbages. Like everyone else Joe and Dorothy began to feel the pinch and their comfortable pre-war lifestyle was now compromised by regulation, order and discipline. Petrol shortages had driven people onto the trains and the evacuation programme to move more than three million children to safety by train had commenced, making commuting from Epsom into London difficult. Joe's responsibilities meant that he had to be on hand to ensure that the paper met its publishing deadline, and so the decision was taken to close down the Epsom house.

Joe often spent the night sleeping in the newspaper's office and he recalled the dark days and nights in London when the dread of bombing was secondary to the fear that the paper might not go to press and the mighty clamouring of the printing machines would be stilled. Black-out conditions had to be maintained at all times; all windows, skylights and glazed doors had to be screened with dark blinds or blankets or brown paper pasted on the glass. No outside lights were permitted, including streetlights. All able-bodied people had to join the army or engage in work to help the war effort, with vast numbers being sent to work in munitions factories. Rather than work in a factory, Dorothy obtained work as a maid in a small Bletchingley hotel, which was owned by two elderly ladies. She and Joe wrote to each other daily and he visited her as often as he could and was always made a great fuss of by the old ladies. Joe had wooed and won Dorothy during the First World War and he had no intention of losing her during the Second World War.

Typically, Joe enlisted in the Home Guard on 14 July 1940, determined to do his duty fending off a familiar foe. Almost two million men, nearly a third of them First World War veterans, volunteered to undertake guard duties, man road blocks and observation points, patrol the streets and report the unusual. But as Joe's 64th birthday approached the hard living started to exacerbate his asthmatic condition. Sleeping rough in the office, working till late at night, taking irregular meals and travelling to see Dorothy, whom he missed all the time, together with the ever-present threat of death, was not the way he had envisaged spending his autumn years. He kept a journal of these difficult times, recording daily experiences and giving an insight into how he managed to balance his work commitments with a meagre social life while trying to maintain contact with Dorothy.

The war entered a more focused phase as Germany recognised that the only way to successfully invade Britain was to gain supremacy in the skies. The Germans launched a sustained campaign, which lasted from August 1940 to late September 1940, in an attempt to destroy the Royal Air Force and ensure easy access to Britain across the English Channel. One massive attack early in September consisted of over 348 German bombers, escorted by more than 600 fighters. Day after day the skies over Britain, and particularly London, were filled with the roar of engines, the chatter of machine guns and the sight of planes trailing plumes of black and white smoke as they plunged from the sky. Occasionally a body could be seen plummeting down and then, as the parachute billowed out, dancing crazily in the sky before gracefully descending to safety.

The Battle of Britain intensified as the Luftwaffe threw more and more resources into the struggle. Bomber planes – Junkers, Stukas and Dorniers – protected by fighter escorts of Messerschmitts, Fockes and Heinkels

dropped bombs from the skies while swarms of British Spitfires and
Hurricanes tried desperately to shoot them down. Britain's pilots,
mostly young men barely into their twenties, fought tenaciously,
and eventually the Germans accepted defeat and gave up their
immediate plans to invade Britain. The battle resulted in the loss
of 900 British planes, and more than 300 pilots out of an
estimated force of 1,000 were killed. Germany's losses were
estimated at more than 1,700 aircraft. Britain's victory gave the
war effort and the civilian population a much-needed boost. The
Prime Minister, Winston Churchill, delivered his epic speech to the
country praising the RAF. 'Never in the field of human conflict was so
much owed by so many to so few.'

Joe Lee in his
Home Guard
uniform, c.1943.

Although defeated in the skies the Germans, in late September, began
the Blitz, which was in effect a campaign to specifically target and bomb
towns and cities. The intention, apart from mass destruction, was to
reduce morale and terrorise civilian populations. London, as the capital,
was the obvious target, but other cities, like Liverpool, Birmingham,
Manchester and Glasgow, were bombed. Coventry was virtually destroyed
on 14 November 1940, and there were more than 1,600 civilian casualties.
The attacks on London started in earnest in September 1940 with daylight
raids. However, the success of strategically placed anti-aircraft guns made
the Germans switch to night bombing raids.

By December 1940 Joe, unsurprisingly, was not happy with his
situation – who was! His meals were taken wherever possible, often using
cafés and restaurants. Lyon's Corner House at Charing Cross was a regular
haunt, where he would on occasion spoil himself with his favourite
kippers for breakfast. Friends often came to his rescue and he fondly
remembers a few days spent with the Brewsters in Redhill. They clearly
lived in some style as they had a serving maid and, at the time of Joe's stay,
were accommodating a few Canadian soldiers. Joe wryly recalled that
when he asked the maid for another egg at breakfast she put him down
with the dry riposte 'You would have to disguise yourself.' The Brewsters
were generous with their hospitality and the quality of the food made a
lasting impression on Joe, whose eating habits were chaotic. A lunch of
veal pie, confit of apples and strawberries and wine merited an entry in

Black Watch Poet Dead

Mr Joseph Lee, well known during the first world war as the Black Watch poet, died at his home, 4 Argyle Place, Thomson Street, Dundee, yesterday after a short illness. He was 71.

A native of Dundee, Mr Lee joined the editorial staff of John Leng & Co., Ltd, in 1909. He was employed in the Aberdeen office in 1914 when war broke out and, along with a number of Dundee colleagues, joined the 1/4th Battalion Black Watch, going overseas in February 1915.

While in the trenches he wrote many poems, which, illustrated by his facile pen, appeared from time to time in the "Dundee Advertiser." They were subsequently published in book form.

Many of the older generation will remember his "Ballads of Battle" and "Work-a-day Warriors."

From the rank of sergeant he received his commission in the King's Royal Rifles, and in December 1917 was taken prisoner.

For 25 years after the war Mr Lee was in journalism in London, retiring several years ago. He returned to Dundee in the autumn of 1947.

He is survived by Mrs Lee, well known as Miss Dorothy Barrie, one of the leading viola players in the country.

Joe Lee put into lines that were sometimes stark the thoughts of the men who fought in the trenches. The "Half-Hour's Furlough" and "Trench Tales" are among well-remembered verses. For example:—

I thought that a man went home last night
  From the trench where the tired men lie,
And walked through the streets of his own old town—
  And I thought that man was I.
As I came by St Mary's Tower
  The old solemn bell struck ten,
And back to me echoed the memory
  Of my boyhood days again.
Musing, I turned me east about
  To the haunt of my fellow men.

So we move on to the last verse:—
Then I awoke to the sound of the guns,
  And in my ears was the cry,
"The second relief will stand to arms."
  And I rose, for that man was I.

Here is a verse from his "Poem of Peace":—

The dawn comes tender as of yore,
  And June is winsome as of old;
The child sings by the cottage door,
  The cuckoo calls from out the wold,
And Winter white is worn to green,
  And fair the daffodill blows—
Even where our reddest blood has been
  The waste will blossom as the rose,
The pennons fly athwart the sky,
  And paeans proud are in the ear—
They are at peace who gave us peace
  And cannot hear.

The obituary which appeared in the paper after Joe Lee's death. It was followed by letters from several admirers of his work.

featured in *Work-a-day Warriors*. Perhaps he wrote it then thinking that the next battle might be his last – happily that was not the case, and Joe Lee had no need of his epitaph until the end of a long and full life. Nevertheless, the second part of the poem summed up his life perfectly, and was still accurate when he died. It epitomises his immense talent as a poet, and eloquently expresses his abiding love of nature and life itself.

EPITAPH

Where the long trench twines snake-like,
  To keep the foe at bay,
There be the place to lay me,
  And this be what you say:

Here lieth one who loved all life,
Sunshine and song, and sword and strife;
Sea and storm, and wind and rain,
Breaking bud, and bursting grain,
Pulsing pleasure, and stabbing pain –
Who would, an he could, live all over again!

Dorothy, at the time of Joe's death, was still a comparatively young woman aged 49, but she never married again. She died in 1992 at the age of 93.

CHAPTER NINE

Famous Encounters

THROUGHOUT his life Lee's work as a reporter, drama critic and sub-editor, together with his great love of the theatre, art and poetry, brought him into contact with some of the theatrical and literary greats during his time in Dundee and London. He first established relationships with some of the leading theatricals when their touring companies appeared at Her Majesty's Theatre, Dundee. Lee would watch the productions, interview some of the leading players and then write a review for the *Dundee Advertiser*. In order to gain favourable reviews some would seek to ingratiate themselves with the drama critics; others, because of their fame and celebrity, would not demean themselves in that way, but one or two, steeped in theatrical tradition, regarded the drama critic as a necessary evil. Lee, with his quiet, unflappable style, appeared to gain the respect and confidence of several of the leading figures of the time.

He formed a particularly warm relationship with the fine English actor, Sir John Martin Harvey. Harvey had first appeared at the London Lyceum with Henry Irving as a young man of 19, and had spent many years learning his craft with the great man. Eventually he graduated into management and toured the provinces with his own Shakespearean productions. However, his reputation as a fine actor owed much to his role as Sydney Carlton in his own production, *The Only Way*, an adaptation of *A Tale of Two Cities*. At the height of his career he was world famous as a romantic actor and manager and was knighted for his services to the theatre. He married Angelita da Silva, who for many years had been his leading lady. Lee had first met him in Dundee and on one occasion

161

travelled to Glasgow to see and report on Harvey in Hamlet. Harvey later wrote to Lee, thanking him for the favourable review.

Although Lee had a great respect for Harvey as an actor and friend, regarding him as particularly gifted with sustained narration, citing as an example the play *The Lowland Wolf*, it was in a private moment that Lee believed Harvey gave one of his finest performances. Joe Lee was home on leave during the First World War when Harvey, who was touring with a production, heard that he was home and invited him to his hotel for lunch. Afterwards they retired to his room for coffee and Harvey, standing by the mantelpiece, started to tell Lee about the letters, some embellished with drawings, that he was receiving from his son who was away fighting on the Western Front. Movingly, unpremeditated and unrehearsed, he spoke passionately about his son and the good times they had enjoyed while he was growing up. He was proud, anxious and worried, and knew that Lee would understand; after all, Lee had survived thus far and was due to return to the fighting. As Harvey spoke from the heart, the drama critic in Lee couldn't help but think that Harvey's eloquent, passionate speech would have made a superb one-act play called *The Boy*, with either a happy or sad ending. Months later, after Lee had been captured by the Germans, he wrote to Harvey to assure him that he was safe. Harvey, in his reply, mentioned with some relief that 'the boy' was recovering in a Cairo hospital. He was hoping to have him home in a few weeks time as he had put him down for Christ Church, Oxford, and the Dean had forwarded his papers to his commanding officer asking for his release in order to continue his studies.

Harvey also gave Lee a list of tour dates for his production for 1918 and invited him to visit him and his wife any time. There was of course the slight complication of Lee being incarcerated in a German prison camp! Commenting on Lee's intention to write a book about his experiences as a prisoner of war, Harvey asked him to send him a copy when it was published, together with some of the beautiful poetry that he used to read in *The Spectator*. Harvey died in 1944 aged 81 years old.

The Terrys, Dame (Alice) Ellen Terry and her brother Fred, were comfortable in Lee's company. Ellen Terry was, at one time, the leading Shakespearean actress in the world. During the period from 1878–1902 her partnership with Henry Irving dominated British and American theatres. In 1903 she embarked on a fresh career, without Irving, in theatre management and lecture tours. She still accepted some acting roles on occasion, and J.M. Barrie and George Bernard Shaw wrote parts especially for her, such as Lady Cicely Waynflete in the 1905 play *Captain Brassbound's Conversion*. Lee remembers an evening spent with her in front of a friendly fireside at a time when she was entering the final period of her stage career, giving a lecture tour on 'Shakespeare's Heroines'. As they chatted he noted that her hard but eloquent mouth still had the knack of breaking easily into a smile. He was fascinated by her large but graceful hands, which she used to great effect, and he understood why audiences were captivated by her. Lee had seen her act with Henry Irving on a number of occasions and she was pleased that he admired her work. Sadly, she told him:

> I might no longer play the parts but I can still discourse about them and to me they have become so living, so lovable that I needs must do it. Shakespearean heroines, Beatrice, Rosalind, Portia, Desdemona, Ophelia, they are all very real to me and I would have the girls of this generation grow to love them as I do.

This interview was the last time that Lee would see Ellen Terry. In 1925 she became a Dame of the British Empire for her services to the theatre and she died in 1928 aged 80.

Her brother Fred became a good friend of Joe Lee, and they met on many occasions. Fred was a fine actor who had also appeared with Henry Irving, but had established himself in the public's eye as Sir Percy Blakeney in *The Scarlet Pimpernel*. A big and breezy character, Terry unfortunately had a heart condition and would usually have a couch in his dressing room on which he would recline while waiting for his cue to go on stage. Lee would sometimes join him in his dressing room to chat and help him relax and pass away the time. On one such occasion Terry confided that after the disastrous production of the *Sword and Song* he totalled the assets of himself and his wife, Julia Neilson, at £300. They were close to ruin and Terry told Lee 'I don't mind confessing that I had a train. Returning to England he began to write, while working as a peddler to get the funds to help publish his poems. In 1907 George Bernard Shaw took an interest in him and arranged the publication of his first work, *A Soul's Destroyer*, which proved to be successful. His autobiography *Super Tramp* followed in 1908 with a continuation, *Beggars,* in 1909, endorsing his early success. Novels and prose including *Adventures of Johnny Walker, Tramp, The True Traveller, A Poet's Pilgrimage* and *Later Days* enhanced his reputation and were followed by a posthumously published volume of poems and lyrics called *Collected Poems* in 1943.

Just after Lee and Davies met, they both had poems published in the same section of *The Nation* and they had mutual respect for each other's work. Besides their poetry, they had both worked in Canada, having travelled across the Atlantic in cattle ships. They would sit and talk in Davies's small room until the early hours about their experiences, art, poetry and the future. However, a neighbour in the adjoining flat was a member of the oldest profession. The music and noise during the comings and goings was not only an indication of her proficiency, but kept Davies awake until the early hours. Despite his remonstrations, she ignored all his pleas for peace and, driven to desperation and knowing that she slept all day following her exertions, he took to banging on her walls. Eventually a tenuous peace was reached.

Davies said that the treasured sketch of himself by Augustus John was made after they had both been dining too well, too long, but not too wisely at the Café Royal. He recalled that they both nearly fell asleep by the fireside as John sketched. Late nights and rich living began to take their toll and Davies admitted that he could not keep up that sort of life either physically or financially, despite the fact that he was now an accepted, collectable poet. Speaking from experience, Davies told Lee that he could do without food, but never without fire and sun. His years of living rough had given him a love for the great outdoors and the ability to cope without luxuries – qualities familiar to Lee. Nevertheless, whenever Lee paid Davies a visit he would always bring him a cake: it was their form of greeting, a breaking of bread. On one occasion Lee called on Davies to find him not at home, but he met him on the street, still chuckling, following a visit to the Alhambra to see the clown Grock. Davies urged Lee to go and see him and Lee later agreed with Davies that Grock was probably the greatest clown of all time.

Davies eventually moved out of London to live in the Sussex countryside, and then moved on to Gloucestershire. Lee would travel out to see him, usually at hawthorn time. They would stroll through the fields and the country lanes, ceasing their chatter from time to time to stop and admire the scenery, with the practised appreciative eye of the poet. Lee's last visit to Davies was in 1938, just after John Masefield, by now the Poet Laureate, had unveiled a plaque at the Old Church House Inn at Newport, Monmouthshire, Davies's birthplace, in recognition of his contribution to British literature. Lee travelled to Nailsworth to see how his old friend was coping with this great honour. It was also an opportunity to interview and sketch him for an article in the *News Chronicle*. As he neared Nailsworth he realised that he had forgotten to bring a cake, and he had to visit a local bakery where he acquired a very poor specimen. Davies greeted him warmly and Joe passed the cake, unseen by Davies, to his wife with a smile. They chatted while Joe sketched and Davies told him that he had been pleased with the honour and the ceremony but remarked that he would have liked to have strolled with Masefield around the docks, to have talked about the ships and the strange sailor-men who used to take him on their knees when he was a tiny boy. However, the little smoking room of the inn had thronged with people who had sat there with Davies's grandfather and his parents and who had remembered Davies as a somewhat loquacious lad, and he had not felt able to make his excuses. While Lee was interviewing Davies, and at the same time trying to make sketches, there suddenly appeared on Lee's sketch book a mysterious red shower, as if from heaven, a sort of miniature plague of Egypt. The culprit was the poet's dog, which had silently entered and shaken its head vigorously. Davies patted him and fondled a ragged, battered ear, remarking, 'Like his master, he enjoys a fight and has had his ear bitten.'

When Joe had finished his sketches, Mrs Davies, a charming dark-eyed Welsh woman, entered with a tea tray, which included Lee's humiliating cake. Davies, not knowing that it was the cake belatedly purchased by his friend, eyed it and commented ruefully 'She does not spoil me'. He continued 'Many poet's wives keep back their adverse criticisms, she takes the hospital to recuperate, following a diagnosis of shell-shock in June 1917. Sassoon was sent to the hospital as part of a compromise arranged by his great friend, another war poet, Captain Robert Graves of the Royal Welsh Fusiliers, to prevent Sassoon being court-martialled for expressing his anti-war views publicly. Sassoon was already famous, because of his stance on the war and his gestures of protest, such as throwing his Military Cross into the River Mersey, and Owen was pleased to make his acquaintance. Sassoon regarded himself as one of the 'Georgian Poets', although his war poems were harsh, cynical and full of rage against authority. Owen, on the other hand, was already an accomplished poet before the war, influenced by Keats and Shelley and drawing inspiration from the Victorian Romantics. His earlier themes of loneliness and angst had already been changing when he met Sassoon, who had a great influence on him, not only introducing him to an exclusive circle of the literary elite, including Edith and Osbert Sitwell, but also offering opportunities for publication, such as in an annual anthology of modern poetry *Wheels* in 1918, and the magazine *The Nation*. Sassoon also helped Owen to change his style, urging him to be more simple, more direct, to try para-rhyme and to draw on his experiences of war for inspiration. *The Nation* published three of Owen's poems and Robert Graves wrote to him calling him a 'damn fine poet'. Owen was thrilled and wrote to his mother telling her that he was now regarded as a peer by the Georgians and declared, 'I am now a poets' poet'. Yet strangely, for all his talent, he wrote his war poetry away from the battlefield. Indeed when writing specifically about conflict he would study others' experiences before writing about his own. A particular source was the French writer, Henri Barbusse, whose accounts of fighting under fire Owen found inspirational. He composed his poems carefully, constructing them precisely, and would often revisit them, restyling them and making alterations, in a way that Joe Lee, writing in the trenches, never did. Sassoon helped him with this process when they were at Craiglockhart together, and the manuscript for perhaps Owen's most famous poem, 'Anthem for Doomed Youth', carries amendments in Sassoon's handwriting. Lee, on the other hand, wrote his poetry in the heat of the moment, shortly before or after an action.

Joe Lee wrote 'Macfarlane's Dugout' during a heavy bombardment, 'At The Dawn' the morning after the battle at Neuve Chapelle, and the to go and see him and Lee later agreed with Davies that Grock was probably the greatest clown of all time.

Davies eventually moved out of London to live in the Sussex countryside, and then moved on to Gloucestershire. Lee would travel out to see him, usually at hawthorn time. They would stroll through the fields and the country lanes, ceasing their chatter from time to time to stop and admire the scenery, with the practised appreciative eye of the poet. Lee's last visit to Davies was in 1938, just after John Masefield, by now the Poet Laureate, had unveiled a plaque at the Old Church House Inn at Newport, Monmouthshire, Davies's birthplace, in recognition of his contribution to British literature. Lee travelled to Nailsworth to see how his old friend was coping with this great honour. It was also an opportunity to interview and sketch him for an article in the *News Chronicle*. As he neared Nailsworth he realised that he had forgotten to bring a cake, and he had to visit a local bakery where he acquired a very poor specimen. Davies greeted him warmly and Joe passed the cake, unseen by Davies, to his wife with a smile. They chatted while Joe sketched and Davies told him that he had been pleased with the honour and the ceremony but remarked that he would have liked to have strolled with Masefield around the docks, to have talked about the ships and the strange sailor-men who used to take him on their knees when he was a tiny boy. However, the little smoking room of the inn had thronged with people who had sat there with Davies's grandfather and his parents and who had remembered Davies as a somewhat loquacious lad, and he had not felt able to make his excuses. While Lee was interviewing Davies, and at the same time trying to make sketches, there suddenly appeared on Lee's sketch book a mysterious red shower, as if from heaven, a sort of miniature plague of Egypt. The culprit was the poet's dog, which had silently entered and shaken its head vigorously. Davies patted him and fondled a ragged, battered ear, remarking, 'Like his master, he enjoys a fight and has had his ear bitten.'

When Joe had finished his sketches, Mrs Davies, a charming dark-eyed Welsh woman, entered with a tea tray, which included Lee's humiliating cake. Davies, not knowing that it was the cake belatedly purchased by his friend, eyed it and commented ruefully 'She does not spoil me'. He continued 'Many poet's wives keep back their adverse criticisms, she takes a delight in hurling them at me, saying there's one in the eye for you.' Her warm smile to Lee underlined the lightness of the moment.

All too soon the visit was over, and Lee remembers Davies's last words as he took leave of him, unknowingly, as it transpired, for the last time. Davies was about to make a broadcast of some of his poems and Lee wished him well. Davies replied 'Oh, I'll be alright if I can only get a couple of glasses of ale inside me.' Lee never saw him again or heard his voice 'save on the air'. He postulated, 'Perhaps some day I shall hear it once more – in the air.'

Following Lee's visit to Davies in 1938, the Second World War made travel more difficult. Lee's job at the *News Chronicle* during the war years was also demanding, which meant that he could rarely leave his post. Sadly his great friend William Henry Davies, the Welsh Tramp Poet, died in 1940 just 18 months after their last meeting. It was almost a replay of the outcome of his friendship with Sir Hugh Walpole; old friends arranging to meet again but having their plans foiled by death.

Of all the Tramp Poet's work, Joe Lee was particularly fond of the poem 'Ambition'.

AMBITION

I had ambition, by which Sir
The Angels fell
I climbed, and step by step, O Lord
Ascended into hell
Returning now to peace and quiet
And made more wise
Let my descent and fall, O Lord
Be into Paradise

Perhaps this poem tells us something more about Joe Lee – it certainly struck a chord with him. Throughout his life and career, Lee was always modest; never thrusting himself into the spotlight, never courting fame or celebrity and, despite his many connections, avoiding the social whirl. He clearly was not, and had never been, an ambitious man, perhaps recognising the pitfalls and penalties of unbridled fame. Nevertheless his talent should have spoken for itself and he should perhaps have been recognised among the very best of the British literary giants. But there may well be other contributing factors that help to explain why Joe Lee was not recognised for his contribution to British literature, and these will be explored in the final chapter in his story.

CHAPTER TEN

A Forgotten War Poet

JOSEPH LEE'S first book of war poems, *Ballads of Battle,* was the starting point for my research into his life and work. I was intrigued by the quality of his work and fascinated by the fact that it had all been produced while on active service in the trenches. It was only when I began to try to find out more about the man that I realised that very little was known about him.

I began my work at my local library, which has an extensive reference section, as well as a particular collection focused on the poetry of the First World War. Starting with the reference section I first of all sought biographical detail. The *Macmillan Guide to Literature,* the *Readers' Companion to 20th Century Writers,* the *Larousse Dictionary of Writers,* the *Cambridge Guide to Literature In English,* the *Bloomsbury Reference Dictionary of English Literature,* the *Reference Guide to English Literature 2nd Edition* and several editions of the *Dictionary of National Biography* were just a few of the reference books I consulted that carried no mention of Joe Lee.

I transferred my attention to the more specific section on First World War Poetry; surely I would find something here. Yet there was nothing in *British and French Writers of The First World War* by Frank Field, or in *Out of Battle – The Poetry of the Great War* by Jon Silkin. *Poetry of The First World War,* selected by Edward Hudson, caught my eye. Thirty-seven poets were featured, with samples of their best work supported by biographical details. It was a superb collection of war poetry. But there was still no mention of Joseph Lee, the Black Watch poet.

At last, in another library in my area, I found a precious reference in

It did of course
Lee was not ap
simple – he wa;
assess style, sy
possibility. How
tained, enthrall
the technical as
been similarly a

Lee's ability a
book of poems,
in 1910. *Ballads*
had three repr
Murray, came c
founded in 176{
It remained in
Headline and t
impeccable tas
published auth
Arthur Conan .
the very best of
been recognise
In 1917 a re|
was published,
advertisement 1
a handful of th¢
Brooke, Capt. I
Sorley and Lieu
By the third
very favourabl

The Time;
fail to hol

The Spec
trenches,

The Columbia-Graingers Index To Poetry, 10th Edition. It listed Joseph Lee as having been born in 1862 (I later discovered that this was incorrect), and having died in 1937 (also incorrect). Two of his poems, 'German Prisoners' and 'The Requiem – When The Last Voyage Ended', were listed, but that was all. Another book, *Never Such Innocence* by Martin Stephen, contained war poetry by 132 poets (68 of whom did not serve in the war), and had a reference to Lee. Again the poem 'German Prisoners' appeared, but this time it was accompanied by some biographical details. It said that Joseph Johnston Lee was born in 1876 and died in 1954 (incorrect), and then gave brief details of his birthplace and war record.

I knew from my edition of *Ballads of Battle* (third print 1917, original print 1916) that Lee had had another book of war poetry, *Work-a-day Warriors* published, and yet here I was struggling to find even the most meagre of references to him. Frustrated, I actually telephoned Edward Hudson, who was responsible for the book *Poetry of the First World War,* and asked him how he could have omitted Joe Lee from his selection of work by 37 poets. He confessed, quite honestly, that he had never heard of Joe Lee.

Despite all my efforts very little information had come to light. Eventually I contacted the archivist of the Black Watch in Perth, Scotland, Thomas Smyth. 'Can you help me?' I pleaded. 'Have you heard of Sergeant Joe Lee?' He replied, 'The Black Watch poet, of course.' Perhaps I should have started my search with the Black Watch in the first place. Thomas then pointed me in the direction of Dundee University and their archives and to my great delight I discovered that they had an extensive archive of material on Joe Lee, including photographs, books, sketches, journals and original manuscripts. As my research continued I received a lot of help and encouragement from Lee's two living relatives, Kathleen Blackwood and Nancy Hughes.

As I started to delve into Joe Lee's background and read more of his excellent work, I became even more bemused by the fact that in the post-war years he had somehow slipped from the notice of the literary world when some of his contemporaries are so well-known, being household names even now, 80 years after the outbreak of the First World War. Occasionally I would search other reference books to assess whether my obsession with his apparent anonymity was justified. Surely there will be the hospital to recuperate, following a diagnosis of shell-shock in June 1917. Sassoon was sent to the hospital as part of a compromise arranged by his great friend, another war poet, Captain Robert Graves of the Royal Welsh Fusiliers, to prevent Sassoon being court-martialled for expressing his anti-war views publicly. Sassoon was already famous, because of his stance on the war and his gestures of protest, such as throwing his Military Cross into the River Mersey, and Owen was pleased to make his acquaintance. Sassoon regarded himself as one of the 'Georgian Poets', although his war poems were harsh, cynical and full of rage against authority. Owen, on the other hand, was already an accomplished poet before the war, influenced by Keats and Shelley and drawing inspiration from the Victorian Romantics. His earlier themes of loneliness and angst had already been changing when he met Sassoon, who had a great influence on him, not only introducing him to an exclusive circle of the literary elite, including Edith and Osbert Sitwell, but also offering opportunities for publication, such as in an annual anthology of modern poetry *Wheels* in 1918, and the magazine *The Nation*. Sassoon also helped Owen to change his style, urging him to be more simple, more direct, to try para-rhyme and to draw on his experiences of war for inspiration. *The Nation* published three of Owen's poems and Robert Graves wrote to him calling him a 'damn fine poet'. Owen was thrilled and wrote to his mother telling her that he was now regarded as a peer by the Georgians and declared, 'I am now a poets' poet'. Yet strangely, for all his talent, he wrote his war poetry away from the battlefield. Indeed when writing specifically about conflict he would study others' experiences before writing about his own. A particular source was the French writer, Henri Barbusse, whose accounts of fighting under fire Owen found inspirational. He composed his poems carefully, constructing them precisely, and would often revisit them, restyling them and making alterations, in a way that Joe Lee, writing in the trenches, never did. Sassoon helped him with this process when they were at Craiglockhart together, and the manuscript for perhaps Owen's most famous poem, 'Anthem for Doomed Youth', carries amendments in Sassoon's handwriting. Lee, on the other hand, wrote his poetry in the heat of the moment, shortly before or after an action.

 Joe Lee wrote 'Macfarlane's Dugout' during a heavy bombardment, 'At The Dawn' the morning after the battle at Neuve Chapelle, and the

Lee's sketch to accompany his poem 'German Prisoners'.

brilliant 'A Shakespeare Tercentenary In The Trenches' 200 yards from the German trenches during a battle in Flanders. The poem includes lines: 'the bullets spat upon the ruined wall' and 'around us were the lodges of our dead'. These are just three examples of the many poems that Lee wrote while on active service on the Western Front. Not for him the comfort of a study, an armchair, a hospital ward, or the luxury of a discussion of style or content with a colleague.

Sassoon was different in temperament to both Lee and Owen; his war poetry was blunt, critical, cynical and unsparing in its targets. In his early days at the front he had supported the war and states chillingly in his book *Memoirs of an Infantry Officer* that he would often go on patrol deliberately seeking a German, any German, to kill. He was at times reckless and was christened 'Mad Jack' by his Royal Welsh Fusiliers comrades. Although he was 'officer class', with his county upbringing, hunting with the hounds, symphony concerts and exclusive literary friends, Lieutenant Sassoon nevertheless cared deeply about his men. It was on their behalf that he raged against authority and those he believed were perpetrating the war for their own ends. His poetry was regarded in some quarters as treasonable and, as mentioned above, there were some who called for him to be court-martialled.

Sassoon returned to France after his spell at Craiglockhart while Owen continued his recuperation in England. In July 1918 he was wounded and invalided out of the war. Owen, after visiting him, was determined to go back to the fighting. In August 1918 he returned to the Western Front and in a brave action in October he was awarded the Military Cross. Within the month, and one week before the war ended, he was killed. In a dreadful irony his parents were notified on Armistice Day, 11 November 1918.

After the war Sassoon took it upon himself to collate Owen's work and most of his war poetry was published posthumously. Whatever the public's feelings about Sassoon and Owen, they were both brave men, both of whom had earned the Military Cross and been unafraid to voice their feelings. They believed that they were protesting on behalf of the 'common men', who had no choice but to fight and who were being slaughtered in their thousands in a badly managed campaign. Their poetry was an expression of the anger they felt about the fate of the common soldier, and the politics of the war in general.

Sassoon's influential friends ensured that his and Owen's poems were widely read. Edmund Blunden, another much-respected poet, stated unequivocally 'Apart from Sassoon, Owen was the greatest English war poet.' A powerful circle of literary figures ensured that this statement went unchallenged.

Joe Lee's poetry of the war, written with a different motivation from that of Sassoon and Owen, was much wider-ranging and diverse. His poems, taken as a whole, are almost a composite history of the First World War. He writes about the bayonet, the rifle, bullets, billets, a mouth-organ, a mother, dugouts, a rifle, leave, home-coming, a nurse, the sea, a carrion crow, the Australians, the Indians and much more. His eye is clearly observant, his brain alert, and he captures the images of the war precisely, both in words and illustrations with his skilled pen and pencil sketches. Added to this he has a range of tone: there are serious poems, humourous poems and lyrical poems that are in the tradition of his beloved Scottish ballads. His offering is certainly different from those of Owen or Sassoon, whose poems centred on suffering, hardship and injustice. Yet they stand at the top of the tree – Lee barely at the foot!

Here, it seems, is one clear reason why Lee's poetry is unknown today; he did not have the powerful backing or support of an influential friend like Sassoon. Joe Lee was neither wounded nor killed in the war, returning after his period in prison in Germany to take up the threads of normal life and go back to working for a living in journalism. Lee had no lofty ambitions of literary greatness and he was reluctant to push himself forward or to exploit his contacts, despite his own circle of talented friends. His preferred lifestyle and character traits no doubt contributed to his low profile after the war. One can imagine what a public relations manager or an agent would today be able to offer Lee, given the tremendous coverage he had had during the First World War.

In 1945 an American from New York wrote to Lee asking for his autograph. Typically Lee, refusing to believe that it was because he was famous, wondered whether it was an attempt at fraud! Nevertheless, even if he had been ambitious and pushy it is doubtful, due to the class distinctions of the time, whether he would have been accepted. Poetry was written by the affluent middle class to be read by the affluent middle class. It was not for factory workers, farm hands, labourers or tradesmen; it was felt that the lower classes did not have either the intelligence or the education to appreciate language, form and style. Some of the poetry written during this time, during the reign of King George V, was published as anthologies or collections of contemporary poetry under the heading of Georgian Poetry. Much of it was romantic, lyrical, and, despite the contributions of some of the younger poets, old-fashioned. Nevertheless, to be associated with the likes of Rupert Brooke, Edmund Blunden, Walter de la Mare, John Masefield, Siegfried Sassoon and Edmund Thomas was considered an honour. No wonder then that Wilfred Owen was overjoyed at being recognised and accepted by the Georgians.

The majority of the poets were Cambridge or Oxford educated. Rupert Brooke went to Cambridge, as did Sassoon, while Robert Graves was at Oxford. Owen, the exception, had the backing of Sassoon and his circle. Edmond Hudson's book, *Poetry of the First World War,* gives a selection of verse from 37 war poets, more than half of whom were Oxford or Cambridge educated. Joseph Lee was from a working-class family, and left school at the age of 14 to start work to help the family survive. Although he was scholarly and widely read he never had the benefit of a lengthy formal education.

Another factor in Joseph Lee's lack of recognition could be called racism. The Scots, before the First World War, did not feel part of British society and on several levels full integration was viewed with scepticism. Indeed the majority of Scots did not want to be part of British society and as a result their contribution, particularly in the field of literature, was negligible. During this era, T.S. Eliot asked, in 1919, rather waspishly, if there was such a thing as Scottish literature. More recently there has been increased interest in what different poetic voices can tell us about experiences – not just different backgrounds, but also different accents, nationalities and persectives. But in the early 20th century Lee may well have been subject to a quiet form of discrimination.

Throughout British history, Scottish soldiers, with great courage, have helped to win and protect British territory all over the world. Their deeds are legendary and well recorded. Nevertheless there has, for centuries, been a love-hate relationship between the English and the Scots. Sometimes it lies dormant and then, as events occur, it once again raises its head. Joseph Lee had, on the face of it, a cordial relationship with

Robert Graves, who had once sent him fraternal greetings in the trenches. Graves, with the Royal Welsh Fusiliers, fought in several areas of the Western Front at the same time as Lee, such as during the action at Festubert. After the war they met in the grounds of John Masefield's house, and at one point they exchanged gifts. In 1921 Robert Graves sent Lee a copy of his *Treasure Box*, inscribed 'To Joseph Lee from Robert Graves, 1921, in gratitude for "The Green Grass". Nevertheless, in his autobiography *Goodbye To All That* Graves is less than complimentary about the qualities of the Scottish soldier. He quotes the opinion of one of his adjutants, admittedly calling it the 'extreme view'. 'The Jocks are all the same, both the trousered kind and the bare-arsed kind, they're dirty in trenches, they skite too much and they charge like hell both ways.' He mentions that his own regiment and the First Middlesex more than once believed that they had been let down by the Scots.

On one occasion when fighting alongside the 10th Highland Light Infantry at Cambrai, the Royal Welsh set up a machine-gun position to cover themselves in case the 'Jocks' ran. Later on in the engagement they did run in panic and were only stopped, at bayonet point, by a sergeant. The position is somewhat balanced in Ian Hay's account of the action in *The First Hundred Thousand* when he states that the Highland Division said that 'the flat caps on the left let them down'. Graves commented, 'I suppose he meant us.'

Regimental rivalry certainly existed and Graves mentioned that if ever a soldier wanted to provoke a fight with the 'Jocks' in a pub all he had to say was 'I'll have a pint of broken square' and the belts would be unbuckled and the fighting would erupt. The phrase 'broken square' refers to the Black Watch, a regiment which Graves must have admired, because he says that even the Black Watch had a blemish. The incident took place at The Battle of Tamaai, where the Black Watch, forming part of the force which tried unsuccessfully to rescue General Gordon at Khartoum, were attacked by the Sudanese, who broke through their famed square formation. The usual rock-solid square was penetrated and great casualties were suffered before the enemy was finally driven off. Detractors said that the square was broken when the soldiers started to retreat, break and run. However, others claim that the incident was caused by confused instructions, not cowardice.

There was also the controversial point that Lee had surrendered his company at Cambrai and had been taken prisoner. Although there was no hint of shame or blame attached to his action, indeed the usual investigation had cleared him of any wrongdoing, it may have been held against him.

The literary group to which Sassoon and Owen belonged was depleted by the war. Rupert Brooke died of blood poisoning while on active service, Wilfred Owen was killed one week before the war ended, and Edmund Thomas and Isaac Rosenberg also died. Sassoon and Edmund Blunden were both invalided out of the war.

It is easy to imagine the tight-knit literary community that was formed in Boars Hill, Oxford, where Robert Graves, John Masefield, Edmund Blunden and the Poet Laureate, Robert Bridges, all lived. Not exactly pro-Scottish, an attitude perhaps reinforced by Dundee's ousting of Winston Churchill as its MP in 1922, they all knew each other very well. Two of them, Graves and Bridges, knew of Joe Lee and his work. Did they never discuss him or consider his work? I find that hard to believe.

Despite Lee's numerous disadvantages: his background, his lack of a literary sponsor and an element of anti-Scottish feeling, perhaps the biggest reason for his consignment to the literary sidelines has its roots in an incident that occured in February 1914, before the war even began.

Lee was particularly inspired by the poetry and songs of his countryman Robert Burns, whose influence can be seen in a number of Lee's poems. In the early part of 1914 Robert Bridges, the newly appointed Poet Laureate, greatly offended Joseph Lee when he wrote 'An Epistle on Instinct' which in Lee's view reproached the 'full-blooded Ayrshire poet in a complacently critical manner'. Bridges wrote:

Robbie Burns.

> Thou art a poet Robbie Burns
> Master of words and witty turns
> Of lilting songs and merry yarns
> Drinking and kissing
> There's much in all thy small concerns
> But more that's missing

He also paradoxically included the line 'There's none can match thee'.

clear indication of frustration at the lack of acceptance and recognition of
Scottish literature by British society.

There follows a magnificent defence of Burns. Lee admonishes Bridges,
writing:

> Robert Burns for all his frailties was too vast a stature to be exhumed
> and dangled like a fully articulated skeleton as a demonstration at an
> anatomy lesson or hung as a moral warning upon a gibbet. We resent
> him as a subject merely for a scientific treatise or a temperance tract.

Lee takes issue with Bridges's last verse, saying that it somehow
conveyed the suggestion of a judicial dismissal with an admonition. Lee is
not swayed by the Poet Laureate's remark that he agrees with R.L.
Stevenson's appraisal of Burns. Lee says that Stevenson admitted much
later in his life that he had underestimated and undermined Burns and
should have spoken out long ago to correct his earlier misconception.
Finally, Lee asks Bridges to forgive him his candour, saying that his
opinion is written not out of malice but from a sense of injustice.

It would take a great deal of understanding to forgive such a detailed,
articulate slap in the face. Robert Bridges did respond in another letter to
Lee, magnanimously to start with. The real resentment was evident,
however, and culminated in a final remark that angered Lee. The Poet
Laureate said that he had liked Lee's 'Poem Expostulating' so much that he
was putting it next to his, so it could be seen! He went on, 'no one is
advantaged by wrong praise and I think that you mistake Burns. His
excellence to which he owes all his fame is surely his marvellous gift of
style – without which he would have been just nothing – while but for the
limitation of his lot it would have set him in the very highest place.' It gets
worse. 'As for you taunting me about the Laureateship – I never did an
unselfish action more unwillingly than when I accepted that office.' He
closes the letter with what Lee describes as an atrocious comment: 'I have
just returned from London where I wasted a day in fitting my Levee suit.
It occurs to me that Burns would have liked that sort of rubbish as
mightily as I loathe it!' Bridges concludes by inviting Lee to meet the
'Anchorite' if he should ever find himself in Oxford. Lee later admitted

that he could not wait to respond and joyfully took up the challenge, bombarding Bridges with testimonials from some of the literary greats. His communication of 22 February 1914, he admits, was a bulky epistle, which left Bridges exhausted, knowing that he had started a fight he could not win. Lee is polite and respectful and then gets down to business with the statement 'You think me mistaken in my estimate of Burns – assuredly one or other of us is. If I am wrong then I am in the very best of company.' He then summons up quotations from the literary world:

Rosetti:	Of all the poets Burns is the most a man
Coleridge:	Burns – Nature's own beloved baird
Byron:	The work of Burns is the very fruit of his art
Lamb:	Burns was the God of my idolatry
Ruskin:	As I grew older and wiser Burns was the influence, from
	Pitt, Charles Kingsley, Matthew Arnold and Tennyson

Lee chastises Bridges for his comment that Burns only had style and nothing else, quoting Walter Scott 'Burns was a wonderful personality,' while others mentioned the vigour of his speech, his conversational prowess and the fact that he was a handsome man with flashing eyes. Lord Roseberry once said of him 'The poetry is only a fragment of Burns.' Lee states that all contemporary testimony is unanimous that Burns, the man, was even more wonderful than his works. Lee takes exception, in his letter, to the comment about the Levee suit, saying that there was no evidence or sanction for it. Burns was usually plainly, almost drably clothed, with meagre resources that could not sustain any desire for more flamboyant dress. The whole correspondence finishes with Lee thanking Bridges for his kind invitation to visit him at Oxford.

Bridges, of course, was not alone in his view of Burns, although his view would seem to be somewhat inconsistent. Having expressed his appreciation of Burns 'There's none can match thee', Bridges nevertheless criticises and almost ridicules the Scottish poet. Although he had a great many devotees, Burns was no middle-class, clean-living privileged poet. He worked on his father's farm, endured hard times, was fond of drinking and fornicating and had, to say the least, a crowded love life. Outspoken and at times difficult, he the red coats and white breeches of the traditional regiments of foot. Very quickly they became known as 'Am Freiceadan Dubh', the Black Watch. However, in 1739 the recruitment of four more companies was authorised, and they were merged with the existing companies to become the 43rd Regiment of Foot. Under the command of Colonel Crawford, the expanded force adopted the red coat and was better known as Crawford's Highlanders. Within the next few years the regiment's sphere of operation was widened to include overseas service, and they fought their first battle against the French at Fontenoy in the War of Austrian Succession in May 1745.

The regiment's return to England coincided with the last Jacobite rebellion. Prince Charles Edward Stuart, Bonnie Prince Charlie, landed in the Hebrides and proclaimed his father James VIII of Scotland, James III of England. Fortified by French and Irish troops he hoped to rally the Highlanders, and indeed the English, in a final rebellion against the House of Hanover. Victory at Prestonpans encouraged an invasion of England, which ground to a halt at Derby. Following his withdrawal to Scotland, he nevertheless again defeated the English in 1746 at the Battle of Falkirk. This victory prompted the arrival in Scotland of the Duke of Cumberland, with a force of sufficient strength to crush once and for all the Jacobite spirit. The armies met at Culloden in 1746 and Cumberland won a decisive victory, so brutal and so ruthless that he was forever known as 'Butcher' Cumberland. At first sight this would seem to be a victory for the English over the Scots. However, closer examination reveals that the 'English' force included many Scots in three regular regiments and two volunteer regiments, while the Jacobite force was bolstered by French and Irish troops. Although there were to be no further rebellions the Jacobite spirit was not extinguished but simmered under the surface.

The Black Watch took no part in any of the battles of the 1745 rebellion. For a short time the regiment served in Ireland, performing a similar function to that for which it was originally created – maintaining peace and order and suppressing signs of rebellion. A period of reorganisation followed and the historically more familiar name of the '42nd Regiment of Foot, The Auld Forty Twa', emerged following a re-numbering exercise, and later the title 'The Royal Highland' was added.

Despite its official listing as 42nd (The Royal Highland) Regiment of Foot (The Black Watch), the more popular name 'The Black Watch' was widely used but would not be officially recognised until more than 100 years later in 1881.

As Britain's influence and power rapidly grew, its various interests and territories came under threat from other nations with global ambitions. The 42nd was despatched to the American colonies to fight the French, who along with Native American tribes were attacking British colonies. Unfortunately, in their only major engagement, attacking Fort Ticonderoga, they were repelled with severe casualties. However they established and laid down a marker, which would characterise the bravery and tenacity of the Black Watch warrior in virtually every other major engagement. With broadsword and bayonet they had attacked a well-defended formidable fortress, without ladders or artillery support, and almost overcome it.

The French were again the enemy in the West Indies in 1758, this time in a successful campaign in Martinique and Guadeloupe. By now the 42nd had two battalions and took on the French in Canada, capturing Quebec and Montreal and ending French rule. Cuba was next on the itinerary as Spain tried to oust the British, before the Black Watch sailed for the American colonies to fight the Native Americans again. When the regiment eventually left America some of the men decided to remain. Some married and established families, while others set up farms or joined other regiments. They sowed the seed for the long traditional link between Scotland and America. In 1776 the 42nd were recalled to America to help put down a revolt against the Crown. They helped capture New York and in a typical Black Watch operation, despite severe losses, they defeated a strong force of Americans at Pisquata. In a night operation near Philadelphia they rushed an American position, guided only by the enemy's campfire, and destroyed the enemy force in hand-to-hand fighting. A period of peace followed, but in Scotland there was some discontent and the Black Watch returned there to keep the peace.

Again trouble in the West Indies towards the end of the 1790s brought action against the French. St Lucia, St Vincent and Trinidad all fell to the 42nd, who then recuperated in Gibraltar, before an attack on Minorca

The Indian Mutiny of 1858 resulted in the 73rd joining the action with
its old 42nd partners. Spells of duty in Britain, Hong Kong, Ceylon and
India followed and then, in 1881, another regimental rethink resulted in
the official title 2nd Battalion Black Watch, and the right to wear the full
Highland uniform, complete with kilt, was reinstated. So from 1881 the
1st Battalion The Black Watch (42nd) and the 2nd Battalion The Black
Watch (73rd) were officially recognised as the Black Watch, although
military records only register the title Royal Highlanders.

Following several years of comparative peace, the first major conflict
saw the 1st Battalion joining the Highland Brigade in defeating the
Egyptians at Tel-El-Kebir. A charge at bayonet point cleared the enemy
lines. The whole of that area was volatile, with the Mahdi, further south,
threatening a full-scale war. The regiment remained in Egypt and the
following year engaged in vicious close-quarter fighting with the Mahdi's
fanatical troops.

Despite successful actions they were unable to get through to Khartoum
to save General Gordon, and it was shortly after a particularly determined
bayonet charge, which cleared the Dervishes from a strong hill-top
position, that news reached the British force of Gordon's defeat and death.
It said much for the strength of character of the Scottish and the rest of the
British forces, that the Dervishes who were regarded as frenzied, fanatical
troops, met their match in close-quarter hand-to-hand fighting. The
bayonet was a fearsome weapon, particularly in skilled and fearless hands.

However it was during the Battle of Tamaai that the Black Watch
suffered its only military blemish. The Dervishes broke the Black Watch
square, inflicting severe casualties before being beaten off. Detractors
allege that the Scots broke under pressure, while others insist that the
chaos was the result of orders being misunderstood. Nevertheless it has
rankled over the years and taunts of 'broken square' have prompted many
a brawl with rival regiments.

Garrison and peace-keeping duties followed for the battalions of the
Black Watch until the Boer War broke out in South Africa in 1899. Once
again it was the 2nd Battalion who linked up with the Highland Brigade
in an attack on a fortified position at Magersfontein. Outsmarted by the
Boers and subjected to 'friendly' fire from their own British artillery,

casualties were severe, and after running out of ammunition retreat was the only option. The Black Watch casualties amounted to over 300 and Magersfontein would be recalled by veterans fighting in the First World War. Greater success was achieved in later battles, contributing to the eventual capitulation of the Boers in 1900. The 1st Battalion joined the 2nd Battalion in South Africa in 1901, helping to police and preserve the peace.

The Black Watch, from its humble beginnings as a Highland police force, had evolved into a much-respected, professional fighting regiment. Its battle honours were global, its troops were garnished with VCs and its reputation throughout the world was second to none. However, greater tests of endurance were only a few short years ahead. Comparative peace for the Black Watch lasted until 1914. The regiment fought with great distinction in the First World War in Belgium, France and Salonika, and suffered 8,000 dead and 20,000 wounded out of an estimated 50,000 regular and territorial serving troops.

Twenty years of stability and home duties followed until 1937 when the 2nd Battalion was engaged in active service in Palestine prior to the outbreak of the Second World War in 1939. It saw action not only in Europe, but also in British Somaliland, Tobruk, El Alamein, Tripoli, India and in the jungles of Burma against the Japanese. At the end of the war the regiment acted as peacekeeper in India as the formation of an independent Pakistan was being brokered and was the last British force to leave Pakistan in 1948.

Yet another major conflict broke out in Korea in 1952 and it was the 1st Battalion The Black Watch, which found itself fighting valiantly against the Chinese. Historically, fighting against superior numbers had never posed a real problem for the Black Watch warrior, and once again they triumphed over the odds. The jungles of Kenya beckoned as the Mau Mau uprising took place in 1953, followed by a short spell of action in Cyprus in 1958 by the 1st Battalion. The Black Watch returned to Cyprus in 1966, once again to keep the peace. Scottish regiments fought in the Falklands War of 1982 and the Gulf War of 1990, but the Black Watch was not engaged in either conflict, but did preside over the handover to China of Hong Kong in 1997.